Effective
Church Growth
STRATEGIES

SWINDOLL
LEADERSHIP
LIBRARY

Effective
Church Growth
STRATEGIES

GENE GETZ & JOE WALL

CHARLES R. SWINDOLL, *General Editor*
ROY B. ZUCK, *Managing Editor*

WORD PUBLISHING
NASHVILLE
A Thomas Nelson Company

EFFECTIVE CHURCH GROWTH STRATEGIES
Swindoll Leadership Library

Unless otherwise indicated, Scripture quotations used in this book are from
the *Holy Bible, New International Version* (NIV),
copyright © 1973, 1978, 1984, International Bible Society.
Used by permission of Zondervan Bible Publishers.

Scripture quotations identified NASB are from the *New American Standard Bible,*
copyright © 1960, 1962, 1963, 1971, 1972, 1973, 1975, 1977, 1999
by the Lockman Foundation. Used by permission.

Unless otherwise indicated, Scripture quotations used in this book are from
the *New King James Version* (NKJV), copyright © 1979, 1980, 1982
by Thomas Nelson, Inc. Used by permission.

Published in association with Dallas Theological Seminary (DTS):

General Editor: Charles R. Swindoll
Managing Editor: Roy B. Zuck

The theological opinions expressed by the authors are not necessarily the official
position of Dallas Theological Seminary.

Library of Congress Cataloging in Publication Data:

Getz, Gene A.
Effective church growth strategies/ Gene A. Getz and Joe Wall
Charles R. Swindoll, general editor
Roy B. Zuck, managing editor
p.   cm.—(Swindoll Leadership Library)
Includes bibliographical references and indexes.

ISBN 0-8499-1363-2

1. Church growth. II. Wall, Joe L. II. Zuck, Roy B. III. Title. IV. Series.
BV652.25.g38 2000
254'5–dc21   99-048665   CIP

Printed in the United States of America
00 01 02 03 04 05 06 BVG 9 8 7 6 5 4 3 2 1

Contents

Acknowledgments

JOE L. WALL

I have been encouraged by the elders and ministerial staff of Cypress Bible Church, Cypress, Texas. Besides supporting me in the writing of this book, they have also joined with me in attempting to implement the principles and ideas suggested in it. The leaders of the church-planting mission in which I serve, East-West Ministries, International, have also been a great encouragement to me, and I am especially indebted to the director of our Central Asia team, Lew Worrad, and his wife, Marguerite, for their discerning personal insights and editorial comments on the book I also would like to acknowledge Bill Bright, founder and president of Campus Crusade for Christ and a world-class visionary, for his impact on my life, and George Peters, late professor of world missions at Dallas Theological Seminary, for stretching my thinking through his provocative insights into the Great Commission. A special thanks is due Marilyn Meyers and Stephanie Fisher for assisting in the typing of one of the drafts. My wife, Linda, has willingly sacrificed many hours of family time to allow me the opportunity to work on this book.

GENE A. GETZ

I would like to thank many people for inspiring me in my church-planting efforts. I'm indebted to Dr. Howard Hendricks, who, as professor of Christian Education at Dallas Theological Seminary, gave me the freedom to explore with my students the concepts and ideas that are unfolded in this book. I'm also grateful to the godly men and their wives who have served with me as lay leaders in founding and establishing a number of churches in the Dallas Metroplex. I'm also deeply appreciative of my wife, Elaine, who has stood by my side during the highs and lows of ministry, always encouraging me to "keep on keeping on." Also I offer a special word of thanks to Iva Morelli, my executive assistant, who typed this manuscript.

Foreword

I'm amazed every time I meet certain people. They seem to believe everything happens by some grand accident. Sometimes they are between jobs, waiting for just the right opportunity. Some are ministers who say, "One day things will start happening around here. Others are students who are waiting until next semester to start a vigorous study program. These folks expect God to work on their behalf without proper planning or personal effort on their own part.

I marvel at the response of some who ask me to pray for them as they look for a job. When I ask, "So how's the job search coming along?" they reply, "It's slow; there's not much out there. Then I normally ask what they are *doing*, what *approach* they are taking in their search. And, to my amazement many respond, "Well, I'm just waiting for an open door." They send out no resumés; they make no phone calls. There's a special term for those who take this I'm-just-waiting approach; it's *unemployed.*

Does the Lord open up incredible doors of opportunity? Yes. Can God work in sudden, amazing ways? Absolutely. However, I've found that He normally blesses hard work and strategic planning. This is His customary way of working.

My longtime friends and colleagues in ministry, Gene Getz and Joe Wall, have written a helpful volume on church growth. This book is filled with practical insights into what it takes to lead a church that is growing and moving ahead. As churchmen, they have spent plenty of time behind the pulpit and inside the board room. They've seen firsthand what works and what doesn't in helping churches grow spiritually and expand numerically. They've both "been there and done that."

I love thinking through the colorful and adventuresome life of the apostle Paul. I'm convinced that he didn't set out on his missionary trips by accident. He had a plan. He had goals he wanted to accomplish, and he had a strategy to reach those goals. If a great leader like Paul had a strategy, shouldn't we? Church leaders who make a difference in their community know where they are going, they know what it will take to get there, and they know how to get others engaged in their mission.

In *Effective Church Growth Strategies* these two seasoned strategists discuss how churches grew in New Testament times, the several factors that contribute toward church growth, the kind of leaders needed to move churches forward, how to assimilate new people into your church, how to start a branch church, how to engage others in the church-growth process. Yet, unlike most church-growth books, Getz and Wall stress that churches grow in numbers as the people grow spiritually. The believers' quality of life, they affirm, is a strong contributor to attracting other people to a church.

I commend this volume to you. I hope you benefit from it as much as I have.

—CHARLES R. SWINDOLL
General Editor

Introduction: Meet the Authors

Dr. Gene Getz and Dr. Joe Wall have both been keenly interested and extensively involved in discovering and communicating principles that reflect a sound, biblical ecclesiology. They have served as pastors of dynamic growing churches and have been actively involved in planting and multiplying churches. And both have ministered overseas on numerous occasions.

Getz and Wall are committed to developing a biblical philosophy of ministry, a process that continually drives their thinking and planning in ministry. They certainly don't claim to have arrived at all the answers, but they are continually in the process of checking their thinking against Scripture.

While committed to the principles of the New Testament, they are also creative and innovative—a freedom they believe grows out of a proper biblical understanding of how to differentiate function from form, principles from patterns, organism from organization, message from methods. In essence, this means understanding the differences between absolutes—those things that should never change—and nonabsolutes, things that may change in order to be both biblical and contemporary.

QUESTIONS THAT NEEDED ANSWERS

In the late 1960s the winds of change that were reflected in the free-speech movement on the West Coast were moving eastward at varying speeds.

These changes were impacting our total culture—including the subcultures in our Christian institutions.

Dr. Getz faced the influences of these changes on the Dallas Theological Seminary campus. Some of his students were asking some very penetrating questions regarding the church and its relevancy in the changing culture. Eager to answer these, Getz took them back to the Scriptures. What does God say about the church? Why does it exist in the world? How should it function in a changing culture? How do we differentiate between absolutes and nonabsolutes? What are the supracultural principles that will work in every culture of the world? How do we avoid becoming institutionalized?

As a result of this process, something dramatic happened. Getz comments, "Unknown to me when I began to explore New Testament concepts of the church with my students, God was preparing me to become a church planter. I never thought I would ever leave the 'sacred halls' of learning where I had spent twenty years as a professor in order to pastor Fellowship Bible Church of Dallas. But I did!"

During this transition from the seminary classroom to the local church, Getz met Joe Wall. Getz initially resisted giving up his full-time professorship. He heard about Wall and his own vision for church planting. Getz and the other elders attempted to convince Wall he should leave his own growing church in Houston, Texas, in order to become senior pastor at the original Fellowship Bible Church, which was growing by leaps and bounds. Though initially interested, Wall declined the invitation, which prompted Getz to face his own future in a new way.

Regarding that watershed moment in his life, Getz explains, "At first, I was very discouraged when Joe turned us down. I wanted to concentrate again on what I had done for twenty years—equipping students for local church ministry. But I rather quickly saw what God was doing in my own life. I had not learned enough about what I was doing—attempting to develop a culturally relevant ministry that was absolutely in tune with the Scriptures. Though the church was growing, I needed far more experience with this new structural model."

When Getz began to devote all his efforts to pastoring, the church grew even more rapidly. In a short time their first building, which seated a maximum of four hundred people, was filled four times each weekend. In the first five years the church leaders planted five branch churches, while the church at the "home base" continued to grow.

Since the original church plant in 1972, Getz has personally started and pastored three of the Fellowship churches in the Dallas area—and helped start nearly a dozen more. One of the most dynamic of these churches is Oak Cliff Bible Fellowship. Tony Evans was a student at Dallas Theological Seminary when Getz began exploring what the New Testament teaches the church should be. Getz challenged Evans to start Oak Cliff Bible Fellowship. The original Fellowship Bible Church provided full financial support for Evans and his family for three years. By then, Oak Cliff Bible Fellowship was able to care for its needs, and today this church is one of the most dynamic churches in the African-American community.

Getz presently pastors the Fellowship Bible Church North in Plano, Texas, which he launched in 1982. The total attendance in Fellowship churches that he directly or indirectly helped start in the Dallas area alone is nearly twenty-five thousand people. In addition, there are more than three hundred Fellowship churches throughout the United States that trace their beginnings back to the Fellowship church movement that began in the Dallas area.

A RELATIONSHIP IS KINDLED

When the elders at the original Fellowship Bible church asked Joe Wall to become senior pastor, he sensed that it was not God's timing. However, a year later Wall moved from Houston to Dallas to work on his doctor's degree at Dallas Theological Seminary and to serve as academic vice-president of Dallas Bible College. At that time Wall and his family joined the original Fellowship church and began to encourage Getz to plant their first mission church—Garland Bible Fellowship. After Wall served as an elder and one of the preaching pastors at the new church and helped them find a permanent location, he decided to return to Houston to once again pastor and stimulate church planting and multiplication in the Texas Gulf Coast region.

Wall served as pastor for fifteen years in the Houston area. He saw God begin to fulfill his dream of a church-planting movement. One church, Spring Branch Community Church, started a number of churches, which in turn started other churches, which continued the process. In ten years the mother church had "great-grandchildren" churches and grew from two hundred and seventy in the mother church to more than eight thousand people in more than twenty-five churches.

In keeping with his commitment to church growth, Wall has pursued other avenues for multiplication during his years as pastor of a church. In the late 1970s he founded the Houston Bible Institute (now known as the College of Biblical Studies of Houston). Since that time, the school has grown to approximately one thousand students with a continuing focus on training minority church leaders.

In 1984, Wall was asked to become the president of Western Bible College in the Denver area. Here he again attempted to apply principles of growth. The college board had been considering closing the school. Building from a student body of approximately 135 students, Wall began to move the school forward through mergers and acquisitions and the addition of creative new programs. First, Western Bible College merged with Rockmont College to form Colorado Christian College. Then Colorado Christian College merged with Colorado Baptist University and acquired a graduate program in biblical counseling under the leadership of Dr. Larry Crabb to form Colorado Christian University. Today approximately three thousand students are enrolled on five campuses.

As the last decade of the 1900s began to unfold, Wall saw the need for training church leaders in the former Soviet Union. Working with Campus Crusade for Christ and then with East-West Ministries, he began to develop schools and training centers—schools that are training church planters and pastors for both Russians and the unreached people groups of Central Asia.

Observing the limitations of traditional educational structures, Wall began to recognize the need to mentor young pastors and church planters, especially those from the former Soviet Union. In 1996, while retaining his training responsibilities in the former Soviet Union with East-West Ministries, Wall again took the pastorate of a church (one that he had planted twenty-five years earlier in Houston). He felt a local church provided a meaningful context for mentoring and training pastors and church planters. At the time of the writing of this book, he is mentoring and training pastors and church planters. He is also engaged in developing a ministry to facilitate cooperative church planting and pastoral mentoring among local Houston churches for both Americans and internationals.

This book, then, combines the biblical and practical insights from two leadering authorities on the planting and growing of churches. Gene Getz has written chapters 2–7, and Joe Wall has written chapters 1, 8, and 9.

—THE EDITORS

1

Thinking Biblically about Church Growth

FLAWED VIEWS OF CHURCH GROWTH

CHURCHES ARE GROWING! In many part of the world people are flocking to churches every Sunday. Church attendance is popular. Why? One reason is that people are searching for spiritual answers to their problems. Another reason is that pastors and other church leaders seem to be giving more attention to church strategies, ways to plant and grow churches.

SOME PASTORS SAY, "I WILL BUILD MY CHURCH"

Although it rarely is stated so crassly, many pastors slide into the trap of thinking about church growth in terms of what *they* can do to make *their* churches grow so everyone will know how successful *they* are. After all, the greater the size and the faster the rate of growth of a church, the more highly esteemed will be the pastor. Size opens doors for pastors to serve on denominational committees and/or boards of Christian organizations. And size makes them sought-after speakers and writers. Church-growth discussions often focus on what church leaders can do differently to bring about significant numerical growth in their churches.

Then church leaders search for ideas and methods that seem to work in other churches. Some try the method of busing children and families to church. Others are attracted to the culturally sensitive philosophy and

1

methods of Willow Creek Community Church in Smith Barrington, Illinois, or Saddleback Community Church in Irvine, California. Still others follow the cell model or the more traditional teaching model. Sometimes true evangelistic growth follows. Other times the efforts flounder and produce division within a church.

SOME CHURCH MEMBERS SAY, "WE WILL MAKE OUR CHURCH COMFORTABLE FOR ME AND MINE"

Most church members are not interested in making their pastor famous or in assuring that their pastor is respected by his peers. They are more concerned that their church is ministering to their children and that their church experiences are enjoyable.

Often church members want to see their church grow so long as it doesn't change too much. They don't want to lose their influence; they like knowing everyone in the church; and they like having a lot in common with most of the people in the church. So when some church members are challenged to give money to help build additional facilities or are encouraged to engage in expanded ministries, they accuse the pastor of being on an ego trip or complain that a focus on local church growth will dilute the church's missionary efforts.

SOME DENOMINATIONAL LEADERS SAY, "WE WILL BUILD OUR DENOMINATION"

Recently I was sitting in a small office in a Moscow high-rise building. My host was the American representative to Russia from a well-known denomination in the States, who had been sent to Moscow to establish a denominational presence. I had met him before and felt sure of his theological soundness, his capability as an expository preacher, and his ability to mentor young Russians.

Our discussion centered on Vitaly, a young Russian who was serving as an intern in his church in Moscow. Because of a long relationship I had with Vitaly, I had asked him and another young Russian to lead a church-planting project in another city. Vitaly was excited about the project, but he wanted to be ordained by the denomination this church was in the process of establishing in Russia. So he asked that I discuss how his pastor, who was also his denominational leader, and I could work together. I agreed, confident that a good arrangement could be made.

The plan was that the church to be planted would be an independent church at first, and then would be free to join any Russian denomination it desired, once it had been established. The possibilities for a cooperative effort seemed good.

But I was dismayed. My host, the denominational leader in Moscow, said that the only way he would agree to ordain Vitaly was for him to make the new church he would plant a member of his denomination from the start. My repeated appeals to consider Vitaly's concerns and the cause of Christ fell on deaf ears—ears apparently muffled by the priority of denominationalism.

Unfortunately some leaders are prone to exalt unduly the importance of their denominations, either consciously or unconsciously.

SOME PARACHURCH LEADERS AND WORKERS SAY, "WE WILL BUILD OUR ORGANIZATION"

Many parachurch organizations were founded by visionary leaders with a passion for evangelism. Often these ministries are more capable of mobility and focus than local churches are. They tend to attract committed believers and often experience more evangelistic success than local churches.

Sometimes workers in aggressive evangelistic parachurch organizations become frustrated with the lack of vision in many churches and their tendency to focus on internal operations. As a result they tend to bypass the local church in their strategic planning and operations. The Great Commission, they believe, is being fulfilled when men and women are won to Christ and have, through a discipleship program, become mature enough to be able to reproduce themselves spiritually. They seem to believe that the local church is a nice option for some involvement, but that the real work is done through parachurch organizations.

Therefore many parachurch strategies for growth do not encourage their constituents to become involved in local churches. Some parachurch staff frequently lead people to Christ and then encourage them to take part in small groups associated with the parachurch ministry. Then in the name of efficiency and for fear of being allied too closely with a particular denomination, church growth is identified with growth in the parachurch organization.

Such thinking became evident at the planning level for the ongoing ministry of CoMission in the former Soviet Union. The CoMission was one of the most impressive displays of selfless cooperation among Christian organizations in this century. More than eighty Christian groups in America and Europe cooperated in developing a plan to evangelize the former Soviet Union. Taking advantage of Campus Crusade's open door to teach Christian ethics in the public schools of the former USSR, a cooperative strategy was developed. It involved personal and group follow-up of schoolteachers by short-term missionaries recruited through most of the participating ministries. The original goal of the project was to plant churches throughout the former Soviet Union. However, any references to church planting had to be deleted from the plans because of Russian Orthodox sensitivities and potential opposition. So the church planting was left to the particular participating mission agency assigned to coordinate the CoMission activities in a specific region.

The next phase of CoMission, called CoMission II, was formed to focus primarily on church planting, taking advantage of the fruit of the evangelism of CoMission I. Other mission agencies, especially those who were committed to church planting and training national leadership for new churches, were invited to join CoMission II. East-West Ministries, the mission agency in which I serve, was invited to join. We were excited about the potential of such a partnership but were soon discouraged by the dominance of some parachurch thinking that made it difficult to use the word *church* in any strategic planning. Instead of speaking about planting "churches," the focus of the strategy was on the planting of "home fellowships," so as not to offend some of the parachurch sensitivities. We continue to look for ways to cooperate with other agencies in CoMission II but find these parachurch prejudices quite limiting.

Solid theological thinking, rooted in biblical concepts, is the best corrective for these and other unhealthy concepts about church growth.

JESUS CHRIST IS THE FOUNDER AND BUILDER OF THE CHURCH

Sometimes we refer to a particular church by the name of the pastor, such as Pastor Brown's church. I remember a mission in West Dallas that had a large sign on the roof announcing that the church was "Brother Bill's Place." Even mainline denominations carry the names of their founders or men who greatly influenced their development—Lutherans, Calvinists, Wesleyans, Mennonites, and others. Jesus, however, taught that there is one church and that He is its Founder and Builder.

When Peter proclaimed who Jesus is, our Lord responded, "Blessed are you, Simon son of Jonah, for this was not revealed to you by man, but by my Father in heaven. And I tell you that you are Peter, and on this rock I will build my church, and the gates of Hades will not overcome it" (Matt. 16:17–18).

Jesus called the universal church *His* church, and later Paul made it clear that this divine ownership could be applied to a particular local church. He and Apollos had both had a part in establishing the church at Corinth (1 Cor. 3:5–10), and he called this church "God's building" and "God's temple" (3:9, 16). Furthermore Paul taught that the source of all true church growth is God: "I planted the seed, Apollos watered it, but God made it grow. So neither he who plants nor he who waters is anything, but only God, who makes things grow" (3:6–7).

The church belongs to Christ, He is the Builder of the church; He is the One who must be given the credit for all true church growth.

THE PRIMARY FOCUS OF CHURCH GROWTH SHOULD ALWAYS BE KINGDOM GROWTH

Too often we take a shortsighted, limited view of our world and miss the larger picture that drives the important issues in life. This is certainly the case when it comes to thinking strategically about church growth. We find ourselves so preoccupied with temporal organizations and human plans that we lose sight of the One this whole endeavor is about.

At the heart of God's purpose and plan for humanity is the kingly rule of His Son. All biblical revelation centers on this glorious reality. Jesus of Nazareth is the promised, anointed King, who will rule the world and bring in the messianic age of righteousness, peace, and prosperity intended by God from the beginning of history for mankind and the earth.

Old Testament Kingdom Expectations

Adam was created to rule, but he failed miserably and the entire human race fell with him. Never did humankind achieve the royal purpose that Moses described in Genesis 1:26, 28, and David wrote about in Psalm 8:6 ("You made him ruler over the works of your hands; you put everything under his feet"). The human race was intended to rule this planet wisely and well under the righteous direction of God. But it has clearly failed. Hebrews 2:8 explains Psalm 8 this way: "In putting everything under him, God left nothing that is not subject to him. Yet at present we do not see everything subject to him." The writer of Hebrews then adds, "But we see Jesus, who was made a little lower than the angels, now crowned with glory and honor" (2:9).

To underscore this great hope and to clarify His plan for the rule of His Son, God established a covenant with David (2 Sam. 7:8–16), in which He made three extraordinary promises: (1) a descendant of David (the Messiah) would be a King who would live forever (an eternal "Seed"); (2) this King would have a government that would have no end (an eternal throne); and (3) His government would rule over the nation of Israel forever (an eternal kingdom).

Many of the Old Testament prophets added exciting descriptions of both the coming King and His glorious rule. They said He would be the virgin-born descendant of King David and He would be worshiped as God—God incarnate, Immanuel. His coming rule on the earth will mean the end of weapons of warfare, injustice, and oppression, and even the physical earth will be changed—the desert will blossom with the rose.

The Kingdom in the New Testament, a Future Hope

In His incarnation Jesus' life was stamped with the claims and evidence of divine royalty. The angel Gabriel declared to the Virgin Mary, "He will be great and will be called the Son of the Most High. The Lord God will give him the throne of his father David, and he will reign over the house of Jacob forever; his kingdom will never end" (Luke 1:32–33). The Magi looked for the "king of the Jews" (Matt. 2:2). John the Baptist preached that the "kingdom of heaven" was at hand (3:1–2). Then Jesus came "proclaiming the good news of God. 'The time has come. . . . The kingdom of God is near. Repent and believe the good news!'" (Mark 1:14–15).

Matthew summarized Jesus' ministry in this way: "Jesus went throughout Galilee, teaching in their synagogues, preaching the good news of the kingdom, and healing every disease and sickness among the people" (Matt. 4:23–25).

Jesus prophesied that this kingdom will come when He returns to the earth: "When the Son of Man comes in his glory, and all the angels with him, he will sit on his throne in heavenly glory. All the nations will be gathered before him, and he will separate the people one from another as a shepherd separates the sheep from the goats. He will put the sheep on his right and the goats on his left. Then the King will say to those on his right, 'Come, you who are blessed by my Father; take your inheritance, the kingdom prepared for you since the creation of the world'" (25:31–34).

After His resurrection His disciples asked Jesus when He would establish Israel's kingdom. Again His response was that the kingdom was yet future. Throughout the Book of Acts the disciples taught about the coming kingdom (Acts 8:12; 14:22; 19:8; 20:25; 28:23, 31).

The kingdom of the Messiah is future, and yet both Jesus and His disciples spoke of the kingdom as though it were present. In Matthew 13 Jesus presented a series of parables to describe the kingdom during the period between His first and second comings. He once told the disciples that the kingdom was present among them (Luke 17:20–21).

Obviously then the Scriptures emphasize two major aspects of Christ's kingdom: His future rule on the earth over every nation and His current rule over His people. In their epistles, both Paul and Peter provided further insight on this subject. Paul taught that all who believe in Christ become members of His body, the church (Eph. 5:29–30), which began on the Day of Pentecost and will end with the Rapture. He also taught that "our citizenship is in heaven. And we eagerly await a Savior from there, the Lord Jesus Christ" (Phil. 3:20). Peter wrote that we are "aliens and strangers" in this present world (1 Pet. 2:11). We are not to try to establish Christ's kingdom in the form of a political state, nor are we to make any church organization synonymous with Christ's kingdom today. But we are to seek to bring men and women to faith in Christ, bringing them "into the kingdom of the Son He loves" (Col. 1:13). This aspect of the kingdom is spiritual (John 3:3, 5), whereas the future form of His kingdom (the Millennium) will be physical, political, and geographical.

In other words, the only time and way the kingdom of Christ will fully become a reality in history is when Jesus comes back wearing the diadem of the King of kings, after having "cleaned house" through His wrathful judgments during the Tribulation, described in Revelation 6–18. Meanwhile He has a large contingency of kingdom citizens who are living as foreigners in a world still dominated by Satan and his minions.

Our relationship to Christ's kingdom can be compared to a group of Americans deciding to move to Russia or China to spread the concept of free enterprise and democracy. They spend their time trying to get the people in the country in which they are living as aliens to join them. Weekly they assemble to encourage each other and sing songs of their American heritage. They carry the "kingdom" of America with them in their hearts, and they remain citizens of a foreign "kingdom." Their weekly assemblies are important and need organization and leadership, but their primary focus is on their allegiance to the country of which they are citizens and for which they labor on foreign soil.

Our Mission: Kingdom Service

The mission of God's people today then is to call people to trust in Christ and thus become citizens of His heavenly kingdom. Local assemblies (churches) are important, and cooperative teams of local assemblies (de-

nominations and fellowships) are helpful. Mobile teams with specific target groups (parachurch ministries) are valid and critical to the success of
our Lord's charge to us. But all these pale in significance in the light of our
identity and calling as citizens of Christ's rule. We are charged as emissaries
of our coming King to bring men and women under His authority now.

Someday every believer will have to stand before the King of the universe, at His special judgment for believers, the "judgment seat of Christ"
(2 Cor. 5:10). Our lives and ministries will be evaluated—especially the
way we have contributed to building Christ's church (1 Cor. 3:10–15). At
that time our Lord will not ask how big our local church was or how
much we contributed to our denomination. He will want to know how
we have invested our lives, our gifts and talents, and our wealth in the
numerical growth of His church and in the spiritual growth of His kingdom citizens.

Local-church leaders, members of our churches, denominational leaders, and parachurch leaders all need to be kingdom-minded and
church-focused. Such people do the following:

- Remain open to creative approaches for "doing church" to better
  reach the lost, even if it means embracing ministries and worship
  services that make them personally feel a bit uncomfortable.
- Look for ways to cooperate with other churches and organizations
  to impact or saturate more effectively their harvest field with the
  gospel.
- Pray for the success of other Christ-honoring churches, denominations, and organizations.
- Do evangelism and discipleship, rejoicing when new disciples find a
  biblical church even if they don't join *their* churches.
- Support plans for planting more churches to reach unreached people
  more effectively, even if it happens to detract from their own church's
  growth.

City-Reaching

Believers who have a vision to reach their communities for Christ in different cities around the world are attempting to develop "city-reaching"

strategies that bring the body of Christ together for more effective evangelistic impact. Leaders of this movement suggest a different, more biblical paradigm for our thinking about the nature of the church. They point out that each of nine of Paul's epistles (Romans through Thessalonians) was written to believers in an entire city. They argue that we need to recover this perspective of seeing local assemblies of believers as part of the larger "church" in our cities. The major spiritual leaders in each city—usually pastors of the more influential churches—need to be identified and encouraged to call believers in the city together for prayer and strategic planning.

The genius of this approach is that it avoids the pitfalls of the ecumenical movement, which promotes church organizational union at the high price of doctrinal compromise. Prayer and strategic planning do not require organizational union. Instead they promote understanding and efficient use of resources. At a large gathering of the church in a given city, the various denominational groups are asked to meet separately to pray and plan how they can contribute to evangelizing the city—church-planting plans, special evangelistic thrusts, and ministries that focus on specific needs in the city. This approach gives churches a way to express the unity that Christ has created in believers and it opens the way for developing powerful cooperative efforts that don't threaten doctrinal purity.

LOCAL CHURCH PLANTING AND GROWTH IS CENTRAL TO ANY STRATEGY TO FULFILL THE GREAT COMMISSION

Few Christians question the crucial importance of the Great Commission of our Lord. However, as they go about the business of evangelism and discipleship, many overlook some extremely critical elements in that commission. For them the growth of the church is simply the adding of disciples to the body of Christ. But a careful examination of the Great Commission and the Book of Acts yields a much larger vision for a truly biblical discipleship ministry.

Jesus' Great Commission is found near the end of three of the four Gospels and in the first chapter of Acts. In Matthew 28:19–20, Jesus commanded His disciples to make more disciples, baptize those new disciples, and then teach them to obey everything He had taught them. In Mark 16:15, Jesus exhorted His followers to preach the gospel to everyone. In Luke 24:46–49, Jesus reminded His disciples that they were witnesses of His death and resurrection, and that they were to preach repentance and forgiveness of sins to all nations, beginning in Jerusalem. Acts 1:8 records a similar statement of the Great Commission, expanding it to include a strategy of an ever-widening circle of witness.

Matthew's account has three major elements that are especially instructive in understanding the relationship of our worldwide mission to the establishing of churches.

Recognizing the Authority of Christ

First, the Great Commission is Christocentric; that is, it is centered in Christ and His authority. Jesus introduced this commission by declaring, "All authority in heaven and on earth has been given to me" (Matt. 28:18). The Commission obviously is connected to His resurrection, by which He has been given authority over everything and everyone in the universe.

However, one might ask, "Hasn't He always had authority over heaven and earth?" Yes, in His deity Jesus has and always will have sovereign authority. However, in His humanity there was a time when He was given authority when, as the Son of David, He was made the royal Heir to the promised messianic kingdom. Jesus, then, it would seem, was announcing the universal authority He had just received from the Father at His resurrection.

Psalm 2:7 refers to the day when God the Father would proclaim to the Messiah that He is His Son (or royal Heir). This prophecy was fulfilled at the resurrection of Christ, as Paul stated in his sermon at Antioch: "Now when they had fulfilled all that was written concerning Him, they took Him down from the tree and laid Him in a tomb. But God raised Him from the dead. . . . God has fulfilled this for us their children, in that He has raised up Jesus. As it is also written in the second Psalm: 'You are My Son, today I have begotten You'" (Acts 13:29–30, 33, NKJV). In other words, at the resurrection of Christ, God the Father pointed to Him and declared that He now had the full rights of a firstborn Heir—Heir to the future throne of David and Heir to the rule of heaven and earth.

Paul introduced his epistle to the Romans with a similar teaching: "Paul, a bondservant of Jesus Christ, called to be an apostle, separated to the gospel of God which He promised before through His prophets in the Holy Scriptures, concerning His Son Jesus Christ our Lord, who was born of the seed of David according to the flesh, and declared to be the Son of God with power according to the Spirit of holiness, by the resurrection from the dead" (Rom. 1:1–4, NKJV).

In another epistle Paul wrote of God's mighty power, "which he exerted in Christ when he raised him from the dead and seated him at his right hand in the heavenly realms, far above all rule and authority, power and dominion, and every title that can be given, not only in the present age but also in the one to come" (Eph. 1:20–21).

According to the Book of Revelation, Jesus has the privileges of the "firstborn from the dead" (Rev. 1:5). Having come forth victoriously from the grave, He has the rights of inheritance, and in His ascended state He is seated at the right hand of God the Father (Eph. 1:20).

Of course, Jesus' authority had already been seen in His earlier commissions to the Twelve and to the seventy. The authority mentioned in Matthew 28:18 was something different, however. This was something grander, with extraordinary ramifications. This was one of the mountain peaks in the history of the universe. Jesus Christ, who was deity in human flesh, had been raised from the dead. And He had been given absolute authority over heaven and earth. That is what the Great Commission is all about. Jesus is Lord of the universe, and we have been commissioned to bring people under His authority. This requires a strategy that includes not only evangelism, but also the establishment of churches, in which believers can be taught how to follow Jesus Christ as their Lord. Is church planting actually implied in the Great Commission? Yes, because, as seen in the Book of Acts, the apostles and others who led people to Christ also organized local churches, in which new believers could find fellowship and be taught God's Word. See, for example, Acts 11:25–26; 14:23, 27; 15:21; 16:5; 18:22; 20:17.

Making Disciples

After His extraordinary declaration of His universal authority in Matthew 28:18, Jesus focused attention on the making of disciples.

What is involved in making disciples? People give different answers to this question. For some, discipleship takes place when we meet with a new believer one-on-one to get him or her started in living the Christian life. Others teach that discipleship involves teaching a particular set of Christian-living principles designed to ground the new believer and equip that person to win others to Christ and disciple them. When one of these insufficient definitions of discipleship is forced onto the Great Commission, much that the local church is called to do is seen as peripheral to the real work of carrying out the Great Commission.

Carefully observing the New Testament use of the term *disciple* sheds light on these erroneous conclusions. It should be noted that in Matthew 28:19–20 Jesus used four verbs to summarize our mandate from Him: *go, make disciples, baptize,* and *teach,* and all but the verb *make disciples* are participles. The primary focus of the verse, then, is on making disciples. *Mathētēs,* the Greek word for *disciple,* can be translated "apprentice" or "learner." A *mathētēs* was one who submitted himself to a master of a particular craft or teacher of a particular view of life in order to learn from him. Thus a *mathētēs* is a "committed follower-learner." It suggests dependence and obedience.

The words *disciple* and *to disciple* are found in all four of the Gospels and a number of times in the Book of Acts (as a synonym for *Christians*),[1] but outside of the Gospels not one of the twelve apostles ever used the term *disciple* in his writings. Although John used the term in the fourth Gospel, the word is not found in any of his three epistles. In addition, neither Paul nor any of the other New Testament writers ever used the term in their epistles.

However, the process of helping believers become maturing committed followers of Christ and developing spiritual leaders is certainly found in the Epistles. Occasionally discipling was a one-on-one process, as seen in the examples of Paul and Timothy, Paul and Titus, and Barnabas and John Mark. And an example of two–on–one discipling is the husband-and-wife team Aquila and Priscilla instructing Apollos. But usually discipling took place in a larger group environment (normally in the context of a church). Paul declared that various spiritual gifts have been given to the body of Christ in local churches to equip believers for involvement in the maturing process of one another *as a team* (Eph. 4:11–16).

Also it is significant that even Jesus seldom met with an individual one-on-one to lead him gradually from faith to spiritual maturity. Rather He had three parts to His discipleship ministry. First, He challenged men and women to follow Him as Lord. He did this in one-time personal encounters and in large-group settings. Second, He provided nurturing for the growth of the committed disciples. Third, He gave special training to selected potential leaders. There is no recorded account of Jesus' nurturing spiritual growth or developing potential leaders through a prolonged one-on-one teaching time. Rather He taught large crowds, a group of twelve, and His inner circle of three. Of course, spending time with an individual for more personal and concentrated training and encouragement can be valuable, but it must never take the place of the healthy functioning of groups.

Based on the centrality of Christ's authority, the use of the term *disciple* in the Great Commission, and the practice of evangelism and church development in Acts, we should expect God's plan for carrying out that commission to focus on the planting of groups of committed disciples of Christ with various spiritual gifts and experience, who can nurture each other. This, of course, strongly implies the multiplication of small groups and the planting of churches.

Baptizing and Teaching

A third major element in the Commission is the inclusion of two additional injunctions: to baptize and to teach all that Christ has commanded. In the Greek "make disciples" is an imperative, followed by two present participles, "baptizing" and "teaching." The participles indicate the *means* by which disciples are to be made. When a person becomes a follower of Christ, that one is to be baptized, thus showing that he or she has become a disciple of Christ. Then the believer grows as a disciple by being continually taught all of Jesus' commands.

Certainly the making of disciples, and even baptizing them, can be done without a local church (for example, Acts 8:36–40), and even some teaching can take place outside a local church. However, the example of the apostolic missionary enterprise in the Book of Acts implies that God intended that churches play a crucial role in carrying out all three of these elements of the Great Commission.

Implementing the Great Commission

The Book of Acts presents an unmistakable picture of the way the first-century missionaries implemented the Great Commission. The Holy Spirit came on the disciples, and the church was born in Jerusalem. The gospel spread throughout the world, and everywhere it went churches were established. The Book of Acts chronicles the establishment of local assemblies of believers in Antioch of Syria, Antioch of Pisidia, Iconium, Lystra, Philippi, Thessalonica, Berea, Corinth, Ephesus, Rome—everywhere the gospel went. The Book of Acts is arranged to show the way the Great Commission was implemented, as is evident by the correlation of Acts 1:8 with the content of the rest of the book. The apostles' witnessing "in Jerusalem" is recorded in Acts 1–7, "in all Judea and Samaria" in Acts 8–12, and "to the ends of the earth" in Acts 13–28.

Of course, the Book of Acts also describes parachurch teams such as Paul's traveling evangelistic teams and his associates and trainees. But even these functioned in such a way that they either planted or strengthened churches. The Great Commission certainly highlights the importance of planting and growing local churches.

What Is a Church?

Is a parachurch ministry a church? Is a small Bible study group in a home or on a university campus a church? Would a parachurch ministry be a church if it practiced baptism and the Lord's Supper?

The Greek word for "church" is *ekklēsia*, which means "assembly." When used in the New Testament to refer to Christians, *ekklēsia* has two connotations: the church universal and the local church. The church universal is also called the body of Christ (Eph. 1:22–23). It is a spiritual organism, consisting of people everywhere who have trusted in the Lord Jesus Christ as their Savior, even if they have not joined a local church. The local church is addressed repeatedly in the salutations of Paul's epistles, and Jesus addressed seven different local churches in Revelation 2 and 3. A local church is a local assembly of professing believers organized to carry out the responsibilities the Scriptures assign to it.

What are the distinctive characteristics of a group of Christians that make it a local church? When does a Bible study group become a church? In teaching pastors and church planters in the former Soviet Union, I have asked them to tell me what they think are the characteristics of a true local church. Usually their list becomes quite long. Different ones suggest that a local church must have elders, deacons, a pastor, a building, government registration, regular meetings, Sunday services, Sunday school, evangelism, teaching, fellowship, prayer, worship, baptism, and the Lord's Supper. But in the discussion that follows, they admit that often churches in the Bible were called churches before they had begun to institute all of these practices. So how do we go about defining a local church?

Three scriptural observations can guide us toward a good definition of a local church. First, the New Testament seems to move readily from references to the universal church to references to local churches (see, for example, 1 Cor. 1:2; 12:27–28; 14:23–33), thus leaving the impression that one is a microcosm of the other.

Second, churches in Acts seem to have consisted of baptized disciples. Normally when a church was formed, it was assumed that its members were disciples (Acts 11:26), and Jesus had indicated in the Great Commission that disciples were expected to be baptized. So the apostles were quick to baptize people who were added to the churches they planted (2:41; 8:13; 10:48; 16:15, 33; 18:8; 19:5), publicly identifying them as disciples of Christ.

Third, the New Testament describes what local churches are to do and how they are normally to be organized, but sometimes they were called churches before they had appointed elders and deacons and before they were able to carry out all the ministries they were charged to do. Therefore we can conclude that *a church is a group of professing believers who have publicly identified themselves by baptism as disciples of Christ and who intend to carry out the functions of a local church.*

What, then, is a church supposed to do? The New Testament mentions four functions:

- To meet regularly (Acts 2:46; Heb. 10:25) as a visible expression of the body of Christ—open to and willing to minister to all believers and their families whatever their age, race, nationality, economic status, or culture (1 Cor. 12:12–13; Gal. 3:26–28; Eph. 2:11–22)
- To be organized under spiritual leadership (Acts 14:23; 1 Tim. 3:1–13; Titus 1:5–9)
- To carry out the basic assembly functions of worship, prayer, teaching, fellowship, caring for the needy, and evangelism (Acts 2:40–47)
- To administer baptism (2:41) and the Lord's Supper (2:46; 1 Cor. 11:23–34).

Believers in a home or college Bible study or believers in a parachurch organization are a part of the universal church. But a Bible study group itself is not a local church, nor is a parachurch ministry a local church. Nor do they constitute the universal church, for that consists of all believers in or out of churches or organizations.

Does this mean that a parachurch ministry that begins a home fellowship in a house cannot call the group a church unless it looks like the traditional church in America? Certainly not. All that a group needs to do to become a church is to commit to function as a church.

Several years ago I was a guest of two Navigator missionaries in Mexico City. One focused on evangelism and small groups on the university campus, and the other was ministering to small groups of graduates who had become a part of the business community. They asked my opinion about creative approaches to "doing church." I suggested that they operate the small groups of university graduates as house churches and that they attempt to multiply the house churches, assigning an elder to one or several of them. The elders could gather all the house churches together monthly for a joint worship service. A number of other models similar to this are flourishing in various parts of the world.

Does the biblical concept of a local church mean that parachurch ministries are not legitimate ministries? No. In fact the New Testament has some examples of parachurch ministries. Paul formed a Bible school in the lecture hall of Tyrannus at Ephesus (Acts 19:9–10). And Paul's traveling missionary team, whose members came from various local churches, certainly functioned as a parachurch ministry.

What are the implications of this brief study of the Great Commission and its focus on the priority of the local church?

- Great Commission-minded local churches and denominations include church planting in their strategies.
- Great Commission-minded parachurch ministries include church growth in their strategies, and they encourage their new converts to be baptized and integrated into local churches.
- Great Commission-minded local churches and parachurch ministries look for ways to partner with each other.

During my ministry of almost forty years, I have been impressed with several prominent examples of men in both parachurch ministries and in local churches who have had such a mind-set. A number of years ago I was invited to have lunch with Lorne Saney, president of the Navigators. I was thrilled to hear him emphasize the importance of the local church in the presence of other Navigator staff. Bill Bright, leader of one of the most effective evangelistic ministries in church history, requires that all his staff join local churches, and he has repeatedly encouraged his staff to partner with churches and to plant churches. In Thailand alone, thousands of churches have sprung up from the evangelistic ministry of Campus Crusade for Christ. I also know of pastors who encourage their people to participate in parachurch ministries, even when it may jeopardize the labor pool within their churches.

FACTORS INVOLVED IN CHURCH GROWTH

Numerical and Spiritual Growth

In discussions on church growth some people focus on activities they hope will produce greater numbers. These activities include new worship styles, evangelistic tools, publicity plans, and the like. Others stress that what is really important is the spiritual growth of believers in the church.

Actually both emphases are biblical. On the one hand, numbering has biblical precedent. An entire book of the Bible bears the name Numbers because the book includes numerical data such as tribal populations and rosters of priests and Levites. When the Lord brought the Jews back from the Babylonian captivity, He recorded the number of people in various families (Ezra 2). On two separate occasions when Jesus fed the multitudes, the Gospel writers reported the number of men who were fed, five thousand and four thousand (Matt. 14:21; 15:38). When the church began on the Day of Pentecost, Luke recorded that three thousand people were saved and baptized (Acts 2:41). Later, an additional five thousand were added to the church (4:4). On numerous occasions large numbers of people, Luke wrote, came to Christ (5:14; 6:1, 7; 9:31; 11:21, 24; 14:1; 17:4, 12; 18:8; 19:26; 21:20). Clearly God is interested in great numbers of people becoming believers!

On the other hand, David received stern discipline from God when he took a census in Israel (2 Sam. 24). Apparently the sin in David's numbering had to do with his improper heart attitude. Joab, the commander of David's army, tried to get the king to reconsider, for he recognized that the numbering was a sign of pride and faithlessness. Apparently David could glory in his power by knowing how numerous his army was.

Keeping up with church membership and attendance can be helpful. Certainly we can use numbers to bring glory to God for His great blessings. Numbers can be helpful in making projections and encouraging momentum in church growth. But we need to be careful that we don't use numbers to glorify our church, our organization, or ourselves, and that we do not replace our reliance on God with trust in our size or numerical growth.

Also numbers can be misleading. Numerical growth may be the result of "transfer growth," that is, attendance may be increasing because believers are transferring their membership from other churches. Thus an increase in members may not necessarily reflect true outreach.

Although concentrating on numerical growth can be valid, it should never eclipse the priority of the spiritual growth of God's people. As we have noticed in the Great Commission, a significant part of our Lord's mandate involves teaching. Ephesians 4:7–16 underscores this purpose of the church. We are to use our spiritual gifts, communicating truth to one another in the context of love, so that we all grow spiritually and become more like the Master.

The Holy Spirit and Wise Planning

Our efforts at church development must recognize both the supernatural working of the Holy Spirit and the wise planning of church leaders.

Without the advantage of modern technology and research, the world was turned upside down in one generation by the early church (Acts 17:6). How did they do it? Actually they didn't. God did, for the Spirit of God supervised the entire movement.

Jesus said the Holy Spirit would come and fuel God's strategic plan: first, Jerusalem, then Judea and Samaria, and then the world (1:8). It was the Holy Spirit who caused the church to explode in one day from an Upper Room prayer meeting of 120 (1:15) to a throng of three thousand (2:41). In response to Peter and John's preaching, it was God who caused the church to grow to five thousand believers (4:4). It was the Holy Spirit who emboldened the entire church to witness in the face of death threats (4:8, 18, 29), and the church continued to grow. It was God who led Peter to the house of Cornelius, a Roman centurion (10:19), when the church stepped through the door leading to a worldwide movement. It was the Holy Spirit who set apart Paul and Barnabas in the church at Antioch for their first missionary journey (13:1–3). It was the Holy Spirit who led Paul across Asia Minor and into Greece (16:6–10). And it was God who sovereignly took Paul through prison and shipwreck to the very courts of the Roman emperor (27:1–28:16).

J. Edwin Orr, a longtime student of revival, has argued that the primary factor behind the major national and international church-growth movements has been the sovereign movement of the Holy Spirit, usually in response to extraordinary prayer on the part of God's people.

No amount of hard work, no creative strategy, no investment of money can produce any true church growth (people coming to Christ and growing spiritually) unless the Spirit of God moves. On the other hand, to acknowledge that church growth is carried out through the guidance and power of the Holy Spirit in no way precludes the involvement of responsible human beings who make informed and wise plans. The Scriptures teach this balance repeatedly.

For example, Psalm 127:1–2 says, "Unless the LORD builds the house, its builders labor in vain. Unless the LORD watches over the city, the watchmen stand guard in vain. In vain you rise early and stay up late, toiling for food to eat—for he grants sleep to those he loves." But the Book of Proverbs also teaches us to work hard (Prov. 6:6–11, 12:11, 27; 13:4, 23). Trusting God is not necessarily contrary to working hard and making wise decisions. The issue is, What is the object of our faith? Are we trusting in our methods and hard work, or are we trusting God? Are our methods the result of prayerfully asking God for guidance, or are they copies of someone else's apparent successes?

Paul and Barnabas were led by the Holy Spirit, but they also normally acted on the basis of wise decisions. Barnabas was from Cyprus, and he had been living in Antioch of Syria. So it would seem wise for their missionary team to go to Cyprus first. Then the closest mainland area to Cyprus was Asia Minor; so Paul, Barnabas, and John Mark sailed to Asia Minor. Later, however, during his second missionary journey, it seemed to Paul that the wisest, most practical strategy would be to go to the Roman province of Asia and its capital, Ephesus. However, the Holy Spirit intervened and led him and his team to Macedonia. Not until his third missionary journey was Paul allowed by the Lord to minister in Ephesus. At that time, he wrote to his Corinthian brothers that God had now opened a door for great and effective ministry in Ephesus (1 Cor. 16:8–9).

We conclude then that growth in a local church depends on the guidance and power of the Holy Spirit, but that the Holy Spirit seeks to use our wisdom and practical plans and actions when they are submitted to the Lord of the church.

2

A Three-Lens Paradigm

WHY IS IT IMPORTANT to develop a biblical, historical, and cultural perspective when planting and growing churches? And why is it necessary to evaluate church forms and structures against the backdrop of biblical principles that emerge from the study of churches in the New Testament?

There are at least two answers to these questions. *First,* if we are to be successful in God's eyes, we must always operate within His will, and it is only in the Scriptures that we can determine His will—in all aspects of life—including the way we do ministry. So we must always look through the lens of Scripture to determine principles that are normative, enduring, cross-cultural, and absolute.

When talking about biblical principles, it's important to understand that these biblical truths do not include the *way* in which these principles are applied in any given cultural situation. Principles relate to activities (functions) and directives (teachings)—not to forms, patterns, and methods. Though it is impossible to engage in *functions* (the application of principles) without some kind of method and structure, it *is* possible to state a principle that describes a function without describing the *form* that principle takes when it is applied. For example, the new believers in Jerusalem "devoted themselves to the apostles' teaching" (Acts 2:42). Here Luke described an activity or function, but the form this took is not described. However, we know there was form and structure because wherever you have people, you have function, and wherever you have function, you have form.

In doing biblical research about the New Testament churches, our challenge is to discover those functions that God wants Christians to be involved in. From those functions, we can develop principles that transcend cultural settings. And if it is indeed a correctly worded biblical principle, it can be applied anywhere in the world, no matter what the societal conditions. Furthermore it is applicable at any moment in history—in the first century as well as in the twenty-first century and any time in between and in the future. This is one fact that sets Christianity apart from all other world religions.

A *second* reason we must develop forms and structures in the light of biblical principles is to avoid being driven by cultural dynamics rather than Scripture. For example, as the megachurch movement gained momentum in the 1980s and 1990s, culture at large moved toward a "shopping mall" approach and mentality. Translated into forms for a large church, this meant providing something for everyone "under the same roof," so to speak. Though this is a noble goal, forms were developed spontaneously that were not in alignment with the core values and structures of the church. In trying to meet people's needs, eventually forms, rather than biblical principles, began to drive the church. In fact, in many instances biblical principles were not clearly thought through and stated. Core values were nebulous. The results were often inefficiency, misunderstandings, vested interests, divisions, wasted resources—and frustrated people.

In many respects this also describes the traditional church. At some point in history, forms were developed to carry out biblical functions and to meet people's needs. However, as culture changed and new needs developed, people refused to change their structures to do a better job of applying scriptural principles in a changing world. They began to serve and perpetuate the structures rather than the reasons these structures came into existence in the first place. This is often called institutionalized religion.

THE LENS OF SCRIPTURE

How do we use the lens of Scripture when developing an adequate philosophy of church planting and growth? To help answer this question, consider the two exhortations in Hebrews 10:25: "Let us not give up meeting together, as some are in the habit of doing, but let us encourage one another—and all the more as you see the Day approaching."

This verse clearly delineates two New Testament directives and functions for the church. Christians are to "meet together regularly" in order to "encourage one another." However, no "form" or "structure" is mentioned in this verse for these two functions. The passage does not specify *when* or *how often* Christians are to meet. Nor are we told *where* to gather or what the *specific order of service* should be when we meet together. Neither does it tell us specifically how we are to "encourage one another."

Differentiating Absolutes from Nonabsolutes

Using this biblical illustration as a model and looking carefully at every activity in the Book of Acts and at every directive in the New Testament letters, we notice three important things.

First, in most cases functions and directives are described in the New Testament without a description of forms—just as we've seen in the Book of Hebrews. For example, Luke recorded that the apostles "never stopped *teaching* and *proclaiming* the good news that Jesus is the Christ" (Acts 5:42, italics added). "Teaching" and "proclaiming" are functions. Though Luke referred to these functions, he did not describe the methods (forms) the apostles followed in their teaching and preaching. However, we know from experience that it is impossible to "teach" and "preach" without some kind of form and method.

Second, when form *is* described in the New Testament, it is always *partial* or *incomplete.* Therefore it is not possible to duplicate biblical form and structure exactly because certain details and elements are always missing in the biblical text. For example, Luke recorded in the same verse (5:42) that the apostles kept right on teaching and preaching as they went "from house to house." Going "from house to house" introduces partial form and structure. In other words, this method is not delineated in detail. Did they stop at every house? Or did they go only to the homes of those who had already believed in Christ? Did people invite their neighbors to come hear the apostles? Did the apostles go inside the house or stand outside? We do not know the answers to these questions because the form described (going "from house to house") is incomplete and partial.

Third, form and structure that is *partially described* also varies from one New Testament setting to another. In fact, we see variations within the text we're looking at. Not only did the apostles teach and preach from house to house, but they also went to the "temple courts" (5:42).

In our culture going from "house to house" may pose a problem immediately. We may not have too much trouble going "from house to house" if we keep the group small. However, if we use the apostles' approach described in the Book of Acts—substituting homes for church buildings— we would probably be in violation of most city ordinances and find ourselves in trouble with local authorities. In fact, violating neighborhood parking restrictions is also a bad Christian witness—the opposite of what God calls us to be. This is why God has given us supracultural principles combined with "freedom in form" in order to apply these principles in every culture of the world.

A Cross-Cultural Experience

The problem of cultural restrictions on Christianity impacted me forcefully a number of years ago when I was sharing principles of New Testament church life in Romania. The Iron Curtain had not yet come crashing down. At that time, it was illegal for groups of people to meet in private homes. Even relatives were not permitted to get together in large numbers. This regulation was not only directed toward Christians, but was established to avoid any potential conspiracy against state authority. Naturally these laws restricted Christians greatly in their ability to use their homes for any kind of religious service involving more than their immediate families. So they were forced by law to meet in church buildings, where their activities could be monitored by communist leaders on a regular basis.

However, as I met with these pastors and discussed the supracultural principle of meeting together regularly, they began to think even more creatively how this could be done in their culture without violating government restrictions. You see, if God had prescribed that the church is to meet in homes, these people would have found it very difficult to do God's will without jeopardizing their own safety.

Don't misunderstand. This does not mean that there will be no times when it is virtually impossible to meet without violating government restrictions. But normally biblical principles allow a great deal of freedom to develop forms to carry out these principles in ways that enable us to do God's will.

These three observations about structure in the New Testament lead to an important hermeneutical principle in determining what is absolute and nonabsolute in Scripture. In essence, it is not possible to absolutize something that is not described. It is always incomplete, and it often changes from one setting to another.

On the other hand, functions and directives yield principles for the church that *are* absolute—*if* they appear consistently throughout New Testament history. This means that we must carefully observe the extent to which New Testament "activities" and "teachings" are repeated, verified, expanded, and reinforced throughout the New Testament. This is what it means to look carefully through the lens of Scripture. It's an exciting, ongoing process and incredibly freeing in being able to do God's work in God's way. Once we understand this process, it enables us to be biblical and yet contemporary.

THE LENS OF HISTORY

We must understand that Scripture *is* history—that is, it's divine history, inspired history, "God-breathed" history. In the pages of the New Testament we discover absolute principles that form the foundation for a biblical philosophy of ministry.

Also we should learn from *all* biblical history, including the Old Testament. Paul made this clear when he wrote 1 Corinthians 10:11: "These things happened to them [the children of Israel] as examples and were written down [in the Old Testament] as warnings for us, on whom the fulfillment of the ages has come."

Today we have not only Old Testament history but also New Testament history—God's divinely inspired history of the church's early years. It too has been recorded for our instruction, to teach us how to lead the church. This, of course, is the lens of Scripture referred to in the previous section.

Church History

Church history is filled with lessons for Christians today. This lens enables us to turn the spotlight on the church in the latter part of the first century and throughout the centuries that followed. This gives us insights that enable us to accentuate what Christians have done correctly, and hopefully will help us eliminate what we've done wrong and correct what we have done poorly. This process, like the study of the church in Scripture, should be an ongoing open-ended activity—enabling us to learn from the past—including our own personal history.

For example, I have helped start a number of Fellowship Bible churches in the Dallas area and have actually pastored three of these churches—building from the ground up. I've learned a lot about church planting—at least in the Dallas area. It would be foolish of me not to utilize this experience to enable me to do a better job each time I've helped plant a church. In fact, Fellowship Bible Church North, where I am senior pastor, has just launched a church in McKinney, Texas—one of our most successful Fellowship Bible churches to date. As of this writing, after only two years, their attendance is moving toward the one thousand mark—not just because McKinney is a growing population center, but because of the year-long process and steps we took to lay the groundwork. Much of what we did was based on lessons from our previous church-planting ministry.

Social History—Fixation, Crisis, and Change

In addition to church history, social history can also offer insights for Christians. Not surprisingly, social historians, who specialize in studying groups of people, have discovered that wherever you have people you have function, and wherever you have function you have form. But they've also discovered several important things about this social dynamic.

First, in studying people and their societal structures, it's obvious people tend to fixate—particularly on forms and structures. People do not want to change their ways of doing things. Put another way, social historians have discovered one constant in history—*fixity*.

However, social studies also reveal that people *do* change their forms and structures in society, basically under one condition—some kind of *crisis*. Only then do people tend to be open to change. Usually a crisis occurs when forms and structures are no longer relevant. They are no longer serving as an effective means to meet the needs of people in that particular society.

In reality, this is what happened when I was teaching full-time at Dallas Theological Seminary in the late 1960s and early 1970s. Reactions against the institutions in our society had spilled over into the Christian community. Secular students particularly had developed an antiinstitutional attitude. They no longer felt their needs were being met—by big government, large universities and colleges, or gigantic corporations. They didn't like becoming what they called a number on an IBM card.

This mentality spilled over into the church community. New Christians particularly—many of whom had been converted on college campuses—began to react to institutionalized Christianity. They felt the forms and structures in the church were no longer relevant to their needs.

This is what precipitated my own in-depth studies of the New Testament church. For the first time as a veteran professor, I changed my game plan in the middle of the courses I was teaching. I knew I had to find answers to the questions my students were asking. Since we all believed that the Bible is the Word of God, we went back to our basic authority. In this process we began to surface absolute principles for a dynamic church life. However, we also learned how important it is to take a look at history. In fact, the lesson that became very significant at that moment is that people do change when forms and structures are no longer relevant in meeting their needs. For me personally, this became the greatest change point in my life—which led me out of teaching into a church-planting ministry.

Why Christians Resist Change

During this process of change in my own life and ministry, I discovered another important insight from history. As Christians, we differ very little from people in general in our psychological makeup. Furthermore, form and structure provide a sense of security. When we tamper with these structures, we're tampering with our emotional stability. This causes anxiety, and anxiety always results in resistance to change.

Let me illustrate this point with another personal experience. When I gave up my role as a full-time professor, which was my life for nearly twenty years—first at Moody Bible Institute and then at Dallas Theological Seminary—I began to experience some unusual anxiety. For a time, I couldn't understand why.

Then one day the reason dawned on me. After years in one kind of structure—a structure I knew very well—I made a dramatic change. We launched a church committed first and foremost to functions and principles. Our goal was to allow the forms and structures to emerge.

From my past experience I knew the forms for a traditional church. I'd been down that road before. I conducted seminars and delivered keynote addresses. But here I was, changing well-known and comfortable academic forms—the seminary classroom—for local-church forms that were basically new and innovative. I hadn't been down that path before, and it created anxiety.

Understanding the source of this anxiety did not solve the problem immediately. However, I understood it and it enabled me to cope with what was normal and predictable. It also made me sensitive to other people. When we make changes in form and structure, we must understand why people resist us. We must help them understand the source of their anxiety.

There is another important lesson Christians must learn. Strange as it might seem, people who have the truth and understand Scripture may have "double trouble" in making changes. Because we believe there are things that should *never change,* we often confuse nonabsolutes (those things that should change) with absolutes (things that should not change). Often this resistance is rooted in insecurity and fear and then leads to rationalization. After all, what better way to rationalize than to *think* we are standing for the truth of Scripture?

On the other hand, many Christians resist change because they are honestly confused. They don't understand the differences between absolutes and nonabsolutes. They put beginning the service with the doxology in the same category as the Virgin Birth. Or they think that meeting at eleven o'clock on Sunday morning is just as significant as what the Bible teaches about the second coming of Christ. Though I'm exaggerating, these illustrations point to our problem.

If we are to experience significant church growth—numerically and spiritually—it's important to understand the difference between absolutes and nonabsolutes, between functions and forms, between principles and patterns, truth and tradition, organism and organization, message and method, the supracultural and the cultural. This is another reason why it's important to look carefully at New Testament churches through the lens of Scripture. But it also illustrates why we need the lens of history, for this helps us discover how Christians in the past succeeded or failed in making these important differentiations.

The Divine Source That Brings Change

Whenever God's truth is taught, it should create a spiritual crisis in the life of every believer who is out of harmony with biblical principles. To be in the will of God, we must change our attitudes and behaviors and conform our lives to God's Word—including the way we do church.

What people learn from Scripture can help them understand God's will for the church. As believers begin to comprehend what is absolute and what is not absolute, what is supracultural and what is cultural, and as they understand that the Bible teaches "freedom in form" in carrying out the Great Commission of our Lord Jesus Christ, most believers will be open to change in areas where they should change. At the same time, they can feel secure in the fact that they are not changing those things God intended to remain the same. Paul's statement to the Corinthians takes on new meaning—"To the Jews I became like a Jew, to win the Jews. . . . To those not having the law I became like one not having the law. . . . I have become all things to all men so that by all possible means I might save some" (1 Cor. 9:20–22). Paul, of course, never compromised his commitment to God's absolutes. Nor did he ever allow himself to get "locked in" to nonabsolutes—the forms, traditions, and rituals of Christianity.

THE LENS OF CULTURE

The lens of culture is also closely related to the lenses of both Scripture and history. We cannot study the Bible without seeing the influence of culture, since all the activities in the New Testament church happened within a given culture. Furthermore, when we study history—particularly social history—we encounter culture.

Jesus carried on His ministry within several cultures, and He understood those cultures well. This was dramatically illustrated when He encountered the Samaritan woman at Jacob's well. Her culture was different from His own. Her viewpoint on religion and life in general differed from that of those who had a typical Jewish background. Jesus used His cultural insights to communicate effectively with this woman. This had a decided effect on how He approached her and taught her divine truth, and on how she responded.

Paul illustrated how important it is to understand culture. We would expect this since his ministry was primarily to the Gentiles, though he was a Jew. As we'll see in a future chapter, his insights into the Greek and Roman cultures actually affected the way he used language—a unique "form" for communicating biblical truth.

The Third Wave

Secular analyst Alvin Toffler has emphasized the influence of culture and why it's important to understand how people think, feel, and act. His book *Future Shock* was a stimulating study on where he believed culture was headed.[1] However, his book *Third Wave* was even more helpful, especially in showing how culture affects form and structure.[2]

Toffler has pointed out that for years much of civilization existed in an agrarian culture—what he calls the "first wave." Societal forms and structures were relatively small because form "conforms" to the number of people involved in any given situation. Generally speaking, this describes the culture in biblical times, though certainly there were exceptions, particularly in the Roman Empire, which boasted some very large cities. Even then, most cultural structures were relatively small, with the exception of the amphitheaters and some religious temples.

Toffler pointed out that much of the world moved from the "agricultural wave" to the "second wave," which he called the "industrial wave." This led to populations being more centralized in large cities and suburbs. These population centers also gave birth to factories, universities, hospitals, and churches. Large forms and structures came into existence to accommodate functions that involved thousands and even millions of people living in a particular geographical area.

The "third wave," which Tofler says is a technological and information era, is of course happening all around us.

Form Always Follows Function

The "industrial wave" gave me a significant cultural insight, particularly in relation to church planting. For a time in my own church-planting experience in the Dallas Metroplex, I (Getz) had determined to keep our church structures small. To achieve this goal, we made multiple use of buildings and started a number of branch churches. However, the more churches we started, the more growth we experienced, primarily because we were in a growing population area. The churches we started in other areas of the city did not resolve the growth problem in our own home-base church.

A couple of things happened that were directly related to culture. First, by having multiple services on Sunday to accommodate everyone who attended, we soon "used up" the culturally acceptable times for worship and teaching periods. Second, in about five years we had exhausted geographical areas of potential places to start new churches. Third, we soon reached the maximum number of people we could accommodate in our own building. Fourth, this began to lead to an "ingrown" mentality—a desire to stop reaching new people. Also, we began turning people away, causing negative feelings on the part of newcomers as well as those who were regulars.

Then I saw that we were beginning to violate the very principles we believed in, and one of those is the maxim that form follows function. To solve these problems, we had to change form—in short, we had to build larger buildings. This, in turn, would affect the form of service. The challenge we faced was to encourage and develop forms that would continue to accommodate the proper function of the church body and would follow other biblical principles.

In summary, I learned that we couldn't force church structures to remain small if we were located in a cultural situation that demanded large structures. Put another way, you can't remain small if you are about the Father's business of reaching people for Christ. And if we are reaching people, we must then design structures to accommodate them in their own cultural environments without violating New Testament principles of church life.

AN ONGOING PROCESS

It is important that we utilize the three-lens paradigm consistently. Forms and structure must change to accommodate church growth. But as we change, we must continually review scriptural principles to be sure we have a correct biblical perspective, and we must utilize lessons from history to make wise judgments in the present. Furthermore, as culture changes, we must adapt to these shifts in mentality without violating biblical principles. If we follow this process, we will be better equipped to develop forms and structures in harmony with God's divine design for the church.

3

Biblical Priorities in Measuring Church Growth

*T*HE PRIMARY BIBLICAL CRITERIA for measuring church growth are clear. The New Testament focuses primarily on *spiritual* growth in the local church, which is best reflected by *faith, hope,* and *love.* Unfortunately, many churches are driven not primarily by these biblical goals but by pragmatic results: numerical growth, buildings, organizational efficiency, the variety of activities, and budget size. Still others single out and focus on a specific biblical function—such as expository preaching, worship, relationships, evangelism, or missions. When one or two of these things are happening, everyone concludes that the church is measuring up to God's standards.

Don't misunderstand. All these functions are good—and necessary. However, a church may be carrying out these biblical functions and practical forms and still be immature. The New Testament teaches that these are means to an end, not ends in themselves. A church's true growth can be measured by the extent to which it is reflecting faith, hope, and love— and especially love. Paul made this point crystal clear when he wrote to the Corinthians: "And now these three remain: faith, hope and love. But the greatest of these is love" (1 Cor. 13:13).

Unfortunately most Christians do not understand the true meaning of this verse of Scripture. Most of us who live in the Western culture have tended to personalize all scriptural teaching. This reflects our cultural mentality—the individualism that permeates our way of living. We often miss the corporate dimensions outlined in Scripture.

Faith, hope, and love represent one of those dimensions. With very few exceptions, New Testament writers used these qualities to measure the maturity level of a local "body" of believers, not just individuals in that body. In fact, many of the New Testament epistles were written to local churches. Take, for example, Paul's two letters to the Thessalonians.

THE THESSALONIAN EPISTLES

After being forced to leave Thessalonica on his second missionary journey, Paul was deeply concerned about the spiritual welfare of the believers he had left behind. When he arrived in Athens, he was so concerned for them that he sent Timothy back to see how they were doing (1 Thess. 3:1–5). When Timothy reported on this trip, he brought good news to Paul, who by then had moved on to Corinth. Evidently Paul immediately penned a letter to these believers (3:6–8). Note how he began this letter: "We always thank God for all of you, mentioning you in our prayers. We continually remember before our God and Father *your work produced by faith, your labor prompted by love, and your endurance inspired by hope* in our Lord Jesus Christ" (1:2–3, italics added).

Besides referring to faith, hope, and love, Paul also indicated how we can measure these qualities in a local church. True faith is reflected in work; true love involves action; and hope that is growing produces stability. The Thessalonian believers—even in the midst of persecution—were reflecting all three qualities. So Paul thanked God as he remembered them in his prayers.

A couple of months later Paul wrote a follow-up letter to this church. It's obvious from the introduction that something had happened in this church. They had become unsettled in their hope, either by "some prophecy" or by a "report or letter" that supposedly had come from Paul and his fellow missionaries (2 Thess. 2:2). The essence of that false information was that these apostolic messengers were teaching that the Day of the Lord had already begun.

This information definitely affected the way Paul began this second letter. He wrote, "We ought always to thank God for you, brothers, and rightly so, because your *faith is growing more and more,* and the *love every one of you has for each other is increasing.* Therefore, among God's churches we boast about your perseverance and faith in all the persecutions and trials you are enduring" (1:3–4, italics added).

Here Paul commended this church for their growth in faith and love, but he said nothing about their hope as he had done in the first letter. Why? The word "hope" in this instance has to do with our confident expectation of the coming of Christ to remove the church from this earth. In Paul's letter to Titus, he called this the "blessed hope—the glorious appearing of our great God and Savior, Jesus Christ" (Titus 2:13).

Evidently a false teacher had taught the Thessalonian believers that Jesus Christ had already come—which definitely affected their spiritual stability. Paul wasted no time in clarifying this issue. He immediately wrote this second letter to reestablish them in their hope.

These believers were growing in their faith and in their love while at the same time they were experiencing insecurity about the return of Christ. This demonstrates that it's possible for a church to be growing in one or two of these qualities and yet languishing in another. Paul was not satisfied until a church reflected all three—faith, hope, and love.

THE TWIN EPISTLES

We see this same pattern in Ephesians and Colossians, Paul's "twin epistles." Though similar in content, there is one major difference. Though written to local churches in Asia, Paul's letter to the Ephesians was probably circular—which explains why there is more reference in this letter to the universal church. The letter to the Colossians was definitely for that particular local church (as well as for the church in Laodicea, Col. 4:16).

In his letter to the Ephesians Paul addressed an issue that was evidently prevalent throughout churches in the province of Asia—which may well have included churches in Smyrna, Pergamum, Thyatira, Sardis, Philadelphia, and Laodicea (Rev. 2:8–3:22). These churches also needed to develop in their hope, but in this instance Paul was referring to another dimension of hope—that of knowing for sure that we have eternal life. "For this reason, ever since I heard about your faith in the Lord Jesus and your love for all the saints, I have not stopped giving thanks for you, remembering you in my prayers. I keep asking that the God of our Lord Jesus Christ, the glorious Father, may give you the Spirit of wisdom and revelation, so that you may know him better. I pray also that the eyes of your heart may be enlightened in order that you may know the hope to which he has called you" (Eph. 1:15–18).

The "hope" Paul was referring to in this letter to the Ephesians related to their security in Jesus Christ. This explains why he began this letter by referring to their eternal position in Jesus Christ:

- God "chose us in him before the creation of the world" (1:4).
- "In love he predestined us to be adopted as his sons through Jesus Christ" (1:4–5).
- "In him we have redemption through his blood, the forgiveness of sins" (1:7).
- "Having believed, you were marked in him with a seal, the promised Holy Spirit" (1:13).

Though the Ephesians were strong in their faith and their love, they needed to be reassured of their hope in Jesus Christ. Once they understood that, they would "no longer be infants, tossed back and forth by the waves, and blown here and there by every wind of teaching and by the cunning and craftiness of men and their deceitful scheming" (4:14).

Though some of the content of Colossians is similar to that of Ephesians, there is one other significant difference. Those believers were presumably more generally mature than the believers Paul addressed in his Ephesian letter. This is why he wrote, "We always thank God, the Father of our Lord Jesus Christ, when we pray for you, because we have heard of *your faith* in Christ Jesus and of *the love* you have for all the saints—the faith and love that spring from *the hope* that is stored up for you in heaven" (Col. 1:3–4, italics added).

THE FIRST CORINTHIAN EPISTLE

What did Paul have in mind when he wrote to the Corinthians, "And now these three remain: faith, hope and love. But the greatest of these is love" (1 Cor. 13:13)?

When he first addressed the Corinthians, he took an entirely different approach. Rather than thanking God for their faith, hope, and love, he thanked God for His grace in their lives. However, it is important to note that Paul was not referring to God's grace that had resulted in their salvation apart from works (see Eph. 2:8–9). Rather, he was attesting to the "grace-gifts" that had been sovereignly bestowed on the Corinthians by the Holy Spirit. The context clarifies what Paul meant: "I always thank God for you because of his grace given you in Christ Jesus. For in him you have been enriched in every way—in all your speaking and in all your knowledge—because our testimony about Christ was confirmed in you. Therefore you do not lack any spiritual gift" (1 Cor. 1:4–7).

Paul was associating God's "grace" with the gifts of the Holy Spirit. However, in spite of their giftedness, the apostle quickly reminded the Corinthians that they had not grown in their Christian lives, even during the eighteen months he had spent ministering to them in Corinth. When he wrote this letter, Paul identified them as "mere infants in Christ" (3:1). They fell far short of being the church God intended them to be. "I gave you milk, not solid food, for you were not yet ready for it. Indeed, you are still not ready. You are still worldly. For since there is jealousy and quarreling among you, are you not worldly? Are you not acting like mere men?" (3:2–3).

Against this backdrop—comparing Paul's use of the words faith, hope, and love in his other epistles—we can now comprehend more quickly and meaningfully what he meant when he referred to these three qualities in 1 Corinthians 13.

As already noted, Paul began this letter to the Corinthians by thanking God for their "grace gifts." The first three verses of chapter 13 returns to this theme. By implication, he acknowledged their possession and use of these gifts, but he reminded them that without love, these gifts were meaningless. In essence, he was saying, "Yes, you have many spiritual gifts, but because you lack love, your gifts are basically useless and certainly do not reflect Christlike maturity."

Their Gifts: Not a Mark of Maturity (1 Cor. 13:1–3)

In these verses Paul wrote, in essence, "If you speak in tongues, but don't have love, then your tongues-speaking would only be noise without true meaning.

If you have the gift of prophecy and great faith, but don't have love, then use of these gifts is meaningless. If you give everything you own to the poor or even surrender your body to the flames, but have not love, you gain nothing of value in God's sight."

We can imagine how the Corinthians were reacting to these indictments on their giftedness—what they thought was a measure of their spirituality. The most painful reality would be to hear Paul suggest that they had no love. Their natural reaction would be to question his words. Anticipating this reaction, the apostle proceeded with a literary technique that must have left them breathless, if not speechless. Within just four verses (13:4–7) he wrote of love in relation to all the major issues he had examined in the first twelve chapters of this letter—issues and problems that demonstrated unequivocally why he concluded they were not demonstrating love in their church.

Their Love: They Had Very Little (1 Cor. 13:4–7)

Love is patient, love is kind. It does not envy. Earlier Paul had said, "You are still worldly. For since there is jealousy and quarreling among you, are you not worldly? Are you not acting like mere men [that is, non–Christians]" (3:3)?

Love does not boast, it is not proud. Earlier Paul had said, "So then, no more boasting about men! . . . Then you will not take pride in one man over against another. . . . What do you have that you did not receive? . . . Some of you have become arrogant, as if I were not coming to you" (3:21; 4:6–7, 18).

Love is not rude. Earlier Paul had written, "It is actually reported that there is sexual immorality among you. . . . And you are proud! . . . Your boasting is not good. . . . When you come together, it is not the Lord's Supper you eat, for as you eat, each of you goes ahead without waiting for anybody else. One remains hungry, another gets drunk" (5:1–2, 6; 11:20–21).

Love is not self-seeking, it is not easily angered. Earlier Paul wrote, "If any of you has a dispute with another, dare he take it before the ungodly for judgment instead of before the saints? . . . But instead, one brother goes to law against another—and this in front of unbelievers! . . . Instead, you yourselves cheat and do wrong, and you do this to your brothers" (6:1, 6, 8).

Love keeps no record of wrongs. Love does not delight in evil but rejoices with the truth. Earlier Paul wrote, "Do you not know that your bodies are members of Christ himself? Shall I then take the members of Christ and unite them with a prostitute? Never! . . . you were bought at a price. There-fore honor God with your body" (6:15, 20).

Love always protects. Earlier Paul had said, "Be careful, however, that the exercise of your freedom does not become a stumbling block to the weak" (8:9).

Love always trusts. Earlier Paul had written, "Am I not free? Am I not an apostle? Have I not seen Jesus our Lord? Are you not the result of my work in the Lord? Even though I may not be an apostle to others, surely I am to you! For you are the seal of my apostleship in the Lord" (9:1–2).

Love always hopes, always perseveres. Later Paul wrote, "And if Christ has not been raised, your faith is futile; you are still in your sins. Then those also who have fallen asleep in Christ are lost. If only for this life we have hope in Christ, we are to be pitied more than all men" (15:17–19).

Following this summary of chapters 1 through 12, and even project-ing ahead to chapter 15, Paul once again returned to their focus—their giftedness—and reminded them that their gifts were merely temporal and were a means of helping develop spiritual maturity in each other. They had allowed their supernatural gifts of grace to become an "end" in them-selves and to become expressions of arrogance and disunity. Paul then explained why love is the greatest of all Christian virtues—even greater than faith and hope.

A Biblical Goal: Pursue Faith, Hope, and Love (1 Cor. 13:8–13)

"Love never fails. But where there are prophecies, they will cease; where there are tongues, they will be stilled; where there is knowledge, it will pass away. For we know in part and we prophesy in part, but when per-fection [your total transformation into the image of Christ] comes, the imperfect disappears. When I was a child, I talked like a child, I thought like a child; I reasoned like a child. When I became a man, I put childish ways behind me. Now we see but a poor reflection as in a mirror; then we shall see face to face. Now I know in part [your knowledge of God is limited], then I shall know fully, even as I am fully known [you will have full knowledge when you are transformed into His image in heaven]. And now these three remain: faith, hope and love. But the greatest of these is love [which was the quality you are missing]. Follow the way of love."

HOW GOD MEASURES MATURITY

As seen in Paul's letters to the Thessalonians, Colossians, Ephesians, and Corinthians, God measures the spiritual maturity of a local church by the degree of faith, hope, and love expressed and reflected by its members. Certainly God's will is that each believer in a corporate body reflect these qualities. Each local church should demonstrate faith, hope, and love—even though in any given church there will be immature believers (new Christians), carnal Christians (those who live after the flesh rather than the Spirit), and even "natural" or unsaved people. In fact, any church that is really impacting the world will include these three groups of people. But at the same time, if the church as a whole is growing in faith, hope, and love, the overall image of that church will be a reflection of Jesus Christ.

All of us involved in helping churches grow need to ask and answer the important questions: If the apostle Paul sat down to write a letter to your church—whether the church is new or not so new, and whether it is small or large—how would he pen the letter? What would he thank God for?

If Paul were to write letters to today's many churches, he would no doubt thank God for a number of things—good attendance, many activities, lovely buildings, organizational efficiency. He might even thank God for great preaching, great worship, great fellowship, and evangelistic activities, and a large foreign-missions budget. However, it's possible to have many or all of these things and not be a church that reflects the spiritual qualities of faith, hope, and love. Only when these three qualities are present can the other elements of church life be as effective as God wants them to be.

4

Three Vital Experiences

TWO BASIC PRIORITIES are essential for church planting, growth, and renewal. The first priority—expressing the spiritually mature qualities of faith, hope, and love—should drive all our activities and functions. As seen in the previous chapter, the church that is maturing is reflecting faith in the Lord, hope in His return, and love for Him and others. Though Paul emphasized this basic value more than any other New Testament author, it is not exclusively Pauline. The author of Hebrews underscored this same core value.

- "Let us draw near to God with a sincere heart in full assurance of *faith*" (Heb. 10:22).
- "Let us hold unswervingly to the *hope* we profess" (10:23).
- "Let us consider how we may spur one another on toward *love* and good deeds" (10:24, italics added in all three verses).

If faith, hope, and love are the marks of a growing and maturing church, then how do we produce these qualities? This leads to the second priority—vital experiences that all Christians need in order to grow in faith, hope, and love. Again, the Bible gives us specific answers. Along with the product, He gives us the process!

Though the process is illustrated numerous times in the Book of Acts and in the Epistles, Luke's record of the spiritual and numerical growth of the church in Jerusalem brings all the necessary ingredients together in one succinct, classic paragraph—Acts 2:42–47. The activities of these New Testament believers can be described and outlined in various ways. But I

(Getz) prefer to identify them as the "three vital experiences." (Many pastors list four experiences vital to the church, by dividing my second category into two parts: fellowship and worship. In fact, Joe Wall, coauthor of this book, holds that view.) These three experiences in turn give us a comprehensive view of what Jesus had in mind when He told the eleven disciples to teach new believers (disciples) to "obey everything" He had taught and "commanded" them (Matt. 28:20).

VITAL LEARNING EXPERIENCES
WITH THE WORD OF GOD

The Holy Spirit came in the midst of "a violent wind" on the Day of Pentecost and enabled the apostles to speak various languages (Acts 2:1–12). Then Peter got up and addressed the crowd (2:14). Quoting from Joel 2 and Psalms 16 and 110, he proclaimed that Jesus Christ is the true Messiah. His Jewish listeners had rejected the very One who had been promised in the Old Testament.

Great conviction fell on the crowd and three thousand people believed in Jesus Christ and were baptized (2:41).

Eager to know more about the Christian faith, "they devoted themselves to the apostles' teaching" (2:42). Ultimately this involved "everything" Jesus had taught them. It's obvious this truth was "unfolded" gradually to the apostles by the Holy Spirit so they could in turn "unfold" God's New Testament revelation to these Jews and others who had become disciples of Jesus Christ (2:5, 41). Just before Jesus was arrested and crucified, He told the apostles in the Upper Room that the Holy Spirit would teach them.

- "All this I have spoken while still with you. But the Counselor, the Holy Spirit, whom the Father will send in my name, will teach you all things and will remind you of everything I have said to you" (John 14:25–26).
- "When the Counselor comes, whom I will send to you from the Father, the Spirit of truth who goes out from the Father, he will testify about me" (15:26).

- "I have much more to say to you, more than you can now bear. But when he, the Spirit of truth, comes, he will guide you into all truth" (16:12–13).

The "truth" the apostles received by direct revelation from "the Spirit of truth" (and which they taught, as seen in the Book of Acts) included what Jesus taught about salvation (for example, His message to Nicodemus regarding the new birth; John 3:1–36), His death, prayer, generosity, worship (for example, His message to the woman of Samaria, 4:19–20), servanthood, and unity. If they had forgotten the content of Jesus' prayer recorded in John 17, the Holy Spirit certainly would have reminded them of that as well.

What Peter and the other apostles began to teach on the Day of Pentecost became the basis of what we now call the New Testament. In His divine plan God has made it possible for believers today to devote themselves "to the apostles' teaching." The New Testament Scriptures contain those doctrines, beautifully and realistically woven into a variety of letters and written reports, many of which were penned directly to New Testament churches and individuals to help them become mature in Christ. These New Testament books enable us to see doctrine in relationship to life experiences, including the problems we face.

The apostles initiated the growth process in the new believers' lives in Jerusalem by exposing them to Bible doctrine. And this process was also carefully followed by the apostle Paul and his fellow missionaries in their church-planting ministry. This is why Paul spent an entire year in Antioch teaching the disciples, a year and six months in Corinth, several weeks in Thessalonica, and three years in Ephesus. This is why he even went beyond a personal ministry among new converts and often sent Timothy and others back to those churches to continue teaching the basic truths of Christianity (1 Cor. 4:17; 1 Thess. 3:2; Titus 2:1).

No church can develop spiritual maturity, reflecting faith, hope, and love, without vital learning experiences with the Word of God. Like the Christians in Jerusalem following their conversion to Jesus Christ, we too must devote ourselves to the apostles' teaching.

VITAL RELATIONAL EXPERIENCES
WITH ONE ANOTHER AND WITH GOD

Besides devoting themselves to "the apostles' teaching," the newborn believers in Jerusalem were also devoted to "fellowship." They were engaged in "the breaking of bread and . . . prayer . . . they gave to anyone as he had need. . . . They broke bread in their homes and ate together with glad and sincere hearts, praising God" (Acts 2:42–47). These verses include four relational activities.

They Ate Together

"Breaking of bread" in many New Testament churches was far more than periodically having a simple communion service, using token elements—a morsel of bread and a sip of juice. Rather, they actually ate a meal together. On occasions, these meals were called "love feasts" (Jude 12; 2 Pet. 2:13). The Corinthians were severely admonished for misusing and abusing this meal (1 Cor. 11:17–34).

These love feasts were no doubt patterned after the Lord's Supper—the final meal which Jesus shared with His disciples before He faced the cross. (Some Bible scholars, however, suggest that the love feast observed in the early church was distinct from the Lord's Supper, and that the love feast either preceded or followed the observance of the Lord's Supper.) During that meal, using the very elements they were eating and drinking together, Jesus broke bread and drank wine, encouraging them to continue to remember His broken body and shed blood in the same way.

The apostles did not then fully comprehend the significance of what Jesus was saying and what they were experiencing. But when the Holy Spirit came at Pentecost, they remembered what Jesus had said and understood what He meant. They took these instructions seriously, and in Jerusalem, it seems that almost every time they had a meal together—as they went from house to house—they were remembering the Lord's broken body and shed blood.

The essence of this experience was fellowship—fellowship with each other as they ate together, and fellowship with Christ as they recalled His death. Here we see a dramatic interrelationship between human relationships and one's relationship with God. As they fellowshipped together around a meal they were also remembering the broken body and shed blood of the Lord Jesus Christ.

Eventually, rather than remembering the Lord with a full meal together, Christians began to observe the Lord's supper by a token meal—a piece of bread and a sip of juice, usually from a common cup that was passed.[1] Today most churches use small individualized cups in practicing this token "meal" in the Lord's Supper.

Again, the form we use for this experience is not the issue. The important thing to remember is that this is to be an experience of fellowship with each other and with God. The quantity of food or even the nature of the elements is not the important issue. What is significant is what happens in the hearts of believers as they enter into this experience.

The form in which the Lord's Supper is observed differs in various cultures. Christians in some parts of the world celebrate the Lord's Supper by passing an ear of corn and each person bites off a few kernels. Then they pass a cup of juice—not necessarily wine or grape juice, but juice from a fruit that is grown in their lands. Obviously God honors the substance—whatever it may be—and the spirit in which Christians enter the experience.

It should be noted that when Christians moved to a "token meal" rather than a "supper," they gave up an important part of this experience—the fellowship that comes from eating a meal together. On the night Jesus was betrayed, He "took bread, and when he had given thanks, he broke it and said, 'This is my body, which is for you; do this in remembrance of me.'" Paul then explained that "after supper," Jesus took the cup and passed it, saying, "This cup is the new covenant in my blood; do this, whenever you drink it, in remembrance of me" (11:23–25). In essence, Jesus began the meal by breaking bread—the bread they were eating. As He passed it, he illustrated that this broken bread represents the way in which His body would be pierced with a sword and His hands and feet would be penetrated and bruised with the nails that pinned Him to the cross. Paul then noted that Jesus partook of a meal. It was called a supper. But as Jesus and the disciples concluded the meal, He took a cup of wine and passed it, stating that this represented His blood that would be shed on the cross.

As believers in the early church and today engage in fellowship and "the breaking of bread" (Acts 2:42), they are eating together while also remembering the Lord Jesus Christ and what He did on the cross.

They Prayed Together

Besides breaking bread from house to house, those early believers also devoted themselves to prayer. This was a unique part of their fellowship together—which leads to another important observation. Prayer among New Testament believers was usually in the context of human relationships. Prayer was a corporate experience.

Of course, this does not mean we should not spend time in personal prayer. However, notice the relational context of prayer in the following passages (italics are added):

- "Be devoted to one another in brotherly love. Honor one another above yourselves. . . . Be joyful in hope, patient in affliction, *faithful in prayer*. Share with God's people who are in need. Practice hospitality" (Rom. 12:10–13).
- "And we urge you, brothers, warn those who are idle, encourage the timid, help the weak, be patient with everyone. Make sure that nobody pays back wrong for wrong, but always try to be kind to each other and to everyone else. Be joyful always; *pray continually*; give thanks in all circumstances, for this is God's will for you in Christ Jesus" (1 Thess. 5:14–18).
- "Is any one of you in trouble? He should pray. Is anyone happy? Let him sing songs of praise. Is any one of you sick? He should call the elders of the church to pray over him and anoint him with oil in the name of the Lord. And the *prayer* offered in faith will make the sick person well; the Lord will raise him up. If he has sinned, he will be forgiven. Therefore confess your sins to each other and *pray for each other* so that you may be healed. The prayer of a righteous man is powerful and effective" (James 5:13–16).
- "The end of all things is near. Therefore be clear minded and self-controlled so that you can *pray*. Above all, love each other deeply, because love covers over a multitude of sins. Offer hospitality to

one another without grumbling. Each one should use whatever gift he has received to serve others, faithfully administering God's grace in its various forms" (1 Pet. 4:7–10).

Just as the communion meal focused on human relationships, which gave this experience meaning and vitality at the divine level, so prayer had two dimensions, both human (addressing human needs) and divine (voicing those concerns to God).

They Shared Their Material Possessions

Giving was also an important part of the fellowship experiences of New Testament Christians. Regarding the church in Jerusalem, Luke wrote, "All the believers were together and had everything in common. Selling their possessions and goods, they gave to anyone as he had need" (Acts 2:44–45).

To comprehend what this meant, we need to understand the unique cultural setting related to their Jewish customs. Every year God-fearing Jews from all over the Roman Empire made a trek to Jerusalem to worship. It was a fifty-day celebration, often involving entire families, and it culminated on the fiftieth day, which they called the Day of Pentecost.

One year on this fiftieth day of the festival, the Holy Spirit descended in Jerusalem and anointed and empowered the apostles, just as Jesus had promised (Acts 1:8). A "violent wind" filled Jerusalem. "Tongues of fire" appeared on the apostles' heads, and these men shared the gospel message in a variety of languages and dialects (2:1–11). These unusual phenomena and Peter's sermon convinced thousands of Jews to place their faith in Jesus Christ, their Messiah. Many Jews who had come from other parts of the Roman world decided to stay on in Jerusalem, even though this was the final day of the Feast of Pentecost.

This decision presented some unusual problems for the apostles. How could they care for the material needs of all these people? However, the problem was resolved when the believers who lived in Jerusalem and in the surrounding areas shared their own material possessions with their brothers and sisters in Christ.

Though the cultural dynamics changed once these Christians understood that it was not God's plan for them to stay in Jerusalem indefinitely, many maintained their unselfish and generous spirit—a true mark of maturity among followers of Jesus Christ. Once believers understand how gracious God has been toward them in giving them the gift of eternal life through His Son, how can they do less than respond by being generous in helping other believers in need?

Note again that this kind of generosity was both a human and divine experience. It was human in that these believers were caring for each other's physical needs. It was divine in that anything that was given to meet the needs of a brother or sister in Christ was blessed by Him. As Jesus once said, "And if anyone gives even a cup of cold water to one of these little ones because he is my disciple, I tell you the truth, he will certainly not lose his reward" (Matt. 10:42).

They Praised God Together

As the believers in Jerusalem participated in these various kinds of fellowship experiences—eating together, praying for one another, and sharing their material possessions—they were also praising God (Acts 2:47). All these activities became means of praise and worship. This too was a part of their dynamic fellowship.

We can safely assume that singing was an intricate part of this praise experience. Jesus modeled this experience when He conducted the Passover meal with His disciples. As Mark noted, "When they had sung a hymn, they went out to the Mount of Olives" (Mark 14:26).

The apostle Paul echoed the importance of this experience in his letters to the Colossians and the Ephesians: "Let the word of Christ dwell in you richly as you teach and admonish one another with all wisdom, and as you sing psalms, hymns and spiritual songs with gratitude in your hearts to God" (Col. 3:16; see also Eph. 5:18–19).

Praising God with song is so interrelated with human relationships that it can't be functionally separated. As they used the medium of music to speak the Word of God to each other, the believers also lifted their voices and hearts in praise and thanksgiving to God. The warm dynamic feelings that were involved in intimate human relationships gave meaning to their relationship with the Lord.

It's clear that these four activities that comprised their "fellowship" experiences were in the context of both human and divine relationships:

- As they ate together, they remembered Jesus' death in the Lord's Supper.
- As they prayed for each other, they fellowshipped with God.
- As they shared their material possessions to meet each other's needs, they were worshiping the one who gave His life for them.
- As they taught each other with psalms, hymns, and spiritual songs, they were lifting their voices in praise and thanksgiving to God.

VITAL WITNESSING EXPERIENCES
WITH THE UNSAVED WORLD

Luke's final statement in Acts 2 about the Jerusalem church demonstrates the impact those believers were having on unconverted Jews, as well as in the lives of God-fearing Greeks who had not yet accepted Jesus Christ as the Messiah. The believers were "enjoying the favor of all the people. And the Lord added to their number daily those who were being saved" (Acts 2:47).

Many of the non-Christians in Jerusalem were impressed with this new corporate lifestyle, this new faith in Christ, this new and vibrant community of love. Therefore many of them listened to the apostles' message, put their faith in Jesus Christ, and joined this growing body of believers.

This dynamic community of love became the most important ingredient that impressed these unbelievers. They communicated the reality of Christ to those who did not know Him. As the unconverted saw these Christians in Jerusalem eating together, praying for one another, sharing their possessions with each other, and praising God, they were deeply impressed. The Jerusalem believers' Christlike lifestyle and mutual love became the bridge that enabled them to share the gospel with people who were willing to listen. They too wanted to know more about the apostles' teaching.

The rapid growth of the church both numerically and spiritually happened because Christ's followers were carrying out the new commandment He gave them in the Upper Room: "A new command I give you: Love one another. . . . By this all men will know that you are my disciples, if you love one another" (John 13:34–35). This phenomenal spiritual response was also a marvelous answer to the prayer Jesus prayed in the presence of His disciples on the way to the Kidron Valley: "My prayer is not for them alone [the apostles]. I pray also for those who will believe in me through their message [the thousands of believers in Jerusalem and throughout history], that all of them may be one, Father, just as you are in me and I am in you. May they also be in us so that the world may believe that you have sent me" (17:20–21).

TYPICAL CHURCH STRUCTURES

What kind of structures does it take to carry out these three biblical functions and to provide believers with these vital experiences? The Bible doesn't specify organizational structures, patterns, and methods in detail. In fact, virtually no structure is included in Acts 2:42–47 in which Luke outlined these activities in the Jerusalem church. This is true throughout the New Testament. We can only speculate about the way first-century Christians did things—or reconstruct from early church history the specific forms and methods they used.

This is by divine design. If the Holy Spirit had detailed the methods by which the New Testament churches functioned, this would have locked us into their culture. And even if it were clear that structures were cultural, our intense desire for a sense of security would cause us to want to imitate those structures. This is why Scripture focuses on directives, exhortations, activities, and functions—the supracultural dimensions of Christianity. These can be duplicated any place in the world, whereas forms, structures, and methods are culturally oriented.

It is also interesting to note how Christians over the years have used this very "freedom in form" to design a variety of structures for the particular vital experience they believe is most important. But we tend to fixate on those very structures, making them absolute and normative. This kind of imbalance and rigidity can lead to serious problems and can keep churches from measuring up to "the fullness of Christ" (Eph. 4:13).

Though admittedly an oversimplification and sometimes overstated, the following observations can help us evaluate what kind of structures we have developed in our own churches to emphasize a particular vital experience.

Churches That Emphasize Bible Teaching

Some churches choose the first vital experience—continuing in "the apostles' teaching" (Acts 2:42). They are often called "Bible-teaching" churches—simply because their emphasis is on teaching the Scriptures. Their structures often reflect the patterns of Bible-teaching institutions (Bible colleges and seminaries) where people are prepared for ministry. For example, pastors tend to function as "teachers" and "professors," and the people in the church are often thought of as "students."

The strength of these churches relates to their theological stability, not being "blown here and there by every wind of teaching" (Eph. 4:14). Their weakness, however, lies in their emphasis on "head knowledge," which is not always translated into their relationships with others, both Christians and non-Christians. Simply learning biblical truths without living them out can easily lead to spiritual pride. As Paul wrote, "Knowledge puffs up" (1 Cor. 8:1).

Some of these churches tend to be nonproductive in reaching people for Jesus Christ. They neglect outreach and evangelism and consequently become ingrown, which eventually leads to internal problems. There is no fresh flow of new life—as in the Jerusalem church—which is such an important factor in maintaining spiritual vitality. Many of these churches are not growing except by transfer of growth from other churches.

Another weakness relates to participation in the local church. Since the focus is on the pastor as a teacher, some members of the church tend to be uninvolved in ministry. And since the people focus on their own personal learning process, they may become preoccupied with themselves rather than reaching out to others.

Churches That Emphasize Relationships

Some churches emphasize the second vital experience—fellowship with one another and with God. Their strength is their warm, accepting environment and local-church participation. There is usually a strong sense of community and love. The people in these churches are often very generous, reaching out to all segments of society.

These churches also have a strong emphasis on worship and praise. Their music focuses on a love relationship with Jesus Christ. Their people tend to have a strong faith in God and what He can do for them and others. Whatever they think the Bible says, they believe. This is a major reason some of these churches are the fastest growing churches in the world.

Their weakness, however, lies in the doctrinal and emotional instability of their membership. Since they are often experience oriented, rather than scripture oriented, they may allow feelings rather than Bible doctrine to take precedence in their decision making. Frequently experience rather than a careful study of the Scriptures dictates what they believe. Furthermore they often sincerely equate emotional experiences with the ministry of the Holy Spirit, believing "ideas" and "thoughts" come from God, whereas they may actually come from themselves. And since they are often weak in the study of the Scriptures, they sometimes follow "experiential" teachings and beliefs that contradict what is taught in the Bible.

Their emotional and spiritual life is also in direct proportion to their relational experiences. They often depend on corporate worship and praise experiences to maintain their spiritual and emotional equilibrium. They find it difficult to "feel good" about their Christian experience unless they are gathered for fellowship with other Christians.

Some of these churches overemphasize the miraculous. People come to depend on "signs and wonders," which leads to an inappropriate focus on human needs and concerns rather than on God's sovereignty and character. Furthermore this emphasis can lead to self-deception, manipulation, and a false simulation of biblical realities. The end result is often disappointment and disillusionment.

Churches That Emphasize Outreach

The major strength of evangelistically oriented churches is their passion to reach people for Christ through preaching and personal witnessing. Sometimes this strength becomes a weakness, for some churches are so involved in winning people to Christ that they do comparatively little to help new converts grow spiritually. The pulpit ministry in these churches is frequently characterized by a diet of evangelistically oriented messages that make the gospel clear but do not edify believers. Regular attenders are often starved for the Word of God, without realizing the cause of this problem.

Many of these churches also tend to operate in an authoritarian manner. The "preacher" is often in control, and even board members may serve only in a "rubber-stamp" position. Sometimes the leaders lack accountability, and the members are often highly motivated by guilt. Some of these groups tend to be highly legalistic in what they believe is spiritual behavior. Many of these people are "busy beavers," engaging in lots of activity and attending numerous church meetings each week. However, many of them have little knowledge of the Bible, since many sermons are topical and repetitive. Also their relationships are often superficial, both within and outside the church.

Within recent years another movement has emerged—often called the "seeker" model for church structures. A number of these churches have rapidly become megachurches. Sunday morning services, designed for unbelievers, emphasize contemporary music, drama, need-oriented messages, and other creative elements. Through unique expressions of "freedom in form" (which the Bible allows and encourages) this approach, if not implemented carefully, can produce "mile-wide" and "inch-thick" churches. That is, commitment and spiritual depth may be lacking. Though characterized by rapid numerical growth, the spiritual life in some of these churches seems to reflect the superficiality and self-oriented lifestyles that permeate much of North American culture.

GOD'S IDEAL PLAN

As stated earlier, these three categories just described are oversimplified and in some instances they may be overstated. Though some churches fit these extreme descriptions, most have a tendency in one direction or another with an imbalanced mixture of all three vital experiences. The fact is that God's ideal plan for every local church is to have structures that provide a healthy balance in all three experiences—just as in the Jerusalem church. When this balance is maintained, then the church can grow in faith, hope, and love.

Building and developing a mature church is both a natural and a supernatural process. The very principles that help build large organizations in the secular world can also help build large churches. However, to produce a church that is spiritually mature and Christlike, the process of church development must be guided, surrounded, and motivated by supernatural principles. Our efforts must be "built on the foundation of the apostles and prophets, with Jesus Christ himself as the chief cornerstone" (Eph. 2:20), and our work must be empowered by the Holy Spirit.

5

Growing a Church with Member Participation

THE CHURCH, THE BODY OF CHRIST, is an organism that is "joined and held together by every supporting ligament" and that "grows and builds itself up in love" (Eph. 4:16).

How can a local body of believers grow and build itself up? By a process that is best described by one New Testament word, *allēlōn,* translated "one another" or "each other." The Epistles often refer to attitudes and actions toward "one another" in a positive sense and other times in a negative sense. The positive items manifest "the fruit of the Spirit" (Gal. 5:22–23), and the negative items manifest "the acts of the sinful nature" (5:19–21). In fact, Paul used the word *allēlōn* in Galatians 5:17 to contrast these two manifestations: "For the sinful nature desires what is contrary to the Spirit, and the Spirit what is contrary to the sinful nature. They are in conflict with *each other*" (italics added).

Here Paul used the "one another" or "each other" concept to show the marked difference between people who follow the "sinful nature" in their relationships with each other and those who "live by the Spirit" and "keep in step with the Spirit" (5:25). Paul was speaking relationally, not just about individual attitudes and actions. This is why he used plural pronouns to describe the way the "acts of the sinful nature" are manifested among non-Christians and the way the "fruit of the Spirit" is reflected in the lives of Christians as they relate to one another.

By grouping the New Testament occurrences of "one another" under "the acts of the sinful nature" and "the fruit of the Spirit," we can see what

Paul had in mind when he stated that these two manifestations are in conflict (5:17).

THE ACTS OF THE SINFUL NATURE

"The acts of the sinful nature are obvious: sexual immorality, impurity and debauchery; idolatry and witchcraft; hatred, discord, jealousy, fits of rage, selfish ambition, dissensions, factions and envy; drunkenness, orgies and the like" (Gal. 5:19–21).

Following is a list of negative "one another" statements that appear in several New Testament letters. Most of these statements are listed as they are translated in the New International Version, but some of them are paraphrased for the sake of consistency or clarity. Note how they reflect the "acts of the sinful nature."

- Lusting for one another (Rom. 1:27)
- Judging one another (14:13)
- Depriving one another (1 Cor. 7:5)
- Biting one another (Gal. 5:15)
- Devouring one another (5:15)
- Destroying one another (5:15)
- Provoking one another (5:26)
- Envying one another (5:26)
- Lying to one another (Col. 3:9)
- Hating one another (Titus 3:3)
- Slandering one another (James 4:11)
- Grumbling against one another (5:9)

THE FRUIT OF THE SPIRIT

"But the fruit of the Spirit is love, joy, peace, patience, kindness, goodness, faithfulness, gentleness and self-control" (Gal. 5:22–23).

The following statements are positive "one another" exhortations. Again, some of them are paraphrased to provide consistency and clarity, but each one reflects what the New Testament authors meant. Notice how these exhortations reflect the fruit of the Spirit.

- Being members of one another (Rom. 12:5)
- Being devoted to one another (12:10)
- Honoring one another (12:10)
- Being of the same mind toward one another (12:16; 15:5)
- Loving one another (13:8; 1 Thess. 3:12; 4:9; 2 Thess. 1:3; Heb. 10:24)
- Edifying one another (Rom. 14:19)
- Accepting one another (15:7)
- Admonishing one another (15:14)
- Greeting one another (16:16; 1 Cor. 16:20; 1 Pet. 5:14)
- Waiting for one another (1 Cor. 11:33)
- Caring for one another (12:25)
- Serving one another (Gal. 5:13)
- Carrying one another's burdens (6:2)
- Bearing with one another (Eph. 4:2; Col. 3:13)
- Being kind to one another (Eph. 4:32)
- Submitting to one another (5:21; 1 Pet. 5:5)
- Esteeming one another (Phil. 2:3)
- Encouraging one another (1 Thess. 4:18; 5:11, 14)
- Confessing sins to one another (James 5:16)
- Praying for one another (5:16)
- Offering hospitality to one another (1 Pet. 4:9)
- Fellowshipping with one another (1 John 1:7)

A church that is manifesting the fruit of the Spirit is practicing the "one another" injunctions that build up the body of Christ and that enable those believers to reflect faith, hope, and love. A church that is reflecting the "acts of the sinful nature" is carnal and is practicing the "one anothers" that keep the church worldly and in a state of carnality. The church in Corinth was like this, for those believers were acting more like non-Christians than Christians. This is what Paul meant when he asked, "Are you not acting like mere men?" (1 Cor. 3:3).

How can a church become a mature body of believers, reflecting faith, hope, and love and other evidences of the fruit of the Spirit? The Scriptures give the answer. All believers must "live by the Spirit" and "keep in step with the Spirit" (Gal. 5:25). And to do this, we must practice the "one another" exhortations that build up the body of Christ (Eph. 4:16) rather than destroying and dismantling it (Gal. 5:15). In no instance are these exhortations qualified, such as "if you feel like it," "if it's convenient," or "if it fits your personality." These exhortations help us see how to do God's will and to please Him. As each believer carries out these positive "one-another" injunctions and avoids the negative "one anothers," a local church becomes more unified, Christlike, and mature. And when that happens, the church may well grow numerically.

The following pages discuss seven of Paul's positive one-another admonitions, all in Romans 12–16.

Members of One Another

"So we, who are many, are one body in Christ, and individually members one of another" (Rom. 12:5, NASB).

The apostle Paul used several metaphors to describe the church. In writing to the Corinthians he used an *agricultural* analogy ("You are God's field") and an *architectural* metaphor (you are "God's building," 1 Cor. 3:9). He added that he had "laid a foundation . . . which is Jesus Christ," and that other spiritual leaders built on this foundation (3:10–11).

In Romans, 1 Corinthians, Ephesians, and Colossians, Paul used an *anatomical* metaphor, one of his most graphic illustrations for the church and one that is exclusively his own in the New Testament. Paul identified God's people as the "body of Christ," using the Greek word *sōma* ("body") more than thirty times. About half of these times he used the word to refer to the human body with its many parts and members, and in the other instances he applied the term to the church, the *body* of Christ.

In all the passages in which Paul used this metaphor to illustrate the church, he emphasized three important principles. The first principle is *interdependence*. No individual Christian can function effectively in isolation and alone. Just as there are many parts of one human body (Rom. 12:4) that work together, so the body of Christ, the church, is made up of many individual members (12:5). And each member is important. We are indeed "members of one another." No member of Christ's body can say to another, "I don't need you," because we all need each other.

The second principle is *humility*. No member of Christ's body should feel more important than any other member of His body. No Christian has exclusive rights to God's grace. Paul emphasized this point in Romans 12:3: "For by the grace given me I say to every one of you: Do not think of yourself more highly than you ought, but rather think of yourself with sober judgment, in accordance with the measure of faith God has given you."

The third principle suggested by the metaphor of the human body is *unity*. Just as the human body has many parts working together, so Christians should work together in harmony. This is why Paul wrote to the Corinthians, "I appeal to you, brothers, in the name of our Lord Jesus Christ, that *all of you agree with one another* so that there may be no divisions among you and that you may be *perfectly united* in mind and thought" (1 Cor. 1:10, italics added). This is why he also wrote to the Ephesians, "Make every effort to keep the unity of the Spirit through the bond of peace" (Eph. 4:3). And to the Romans he said, "Let us therefore make every effort to do what leads to peace and to mutual edification" (Rom. 14:19). Put another way, Paul was exhorting these Christians to do everything they could to "build up one another."

Devoted to One Another

"Be devoted to one another in brotherly love" (Rom. 12:10).

This introduces us to another powerful metaphor for the church. The Greek word *philadelphia*, "brotherly love," refers to family relationships. Applied to the church, Paul was referring to the love that brothers and sisters in Christ should have for each other.

The word *adelphos*, "brother," which is part of the word *philadelphia*, was used by New Testament writers to refer to other Christians more than two hundred times, beginning in the Book of Acts. When this family term is applied to Christians, it means "fellow believers," "members of God's family," "brothers and sisters in Christ," "members of God's household" (Eph. 2:19). It means we have all been "born again" into God's eternal family. Thus we are vitally related to each other through a common heritage. God has "adopted" all of us "as his sons [and daughters] through Jesus Christ" (1:5).

God's "family"—as He designed it to function—helps us appreciate what a healthy church should be. This metaphor adds a dimension of warmth, tenderness, concern, and loyalty—in short, human emotion and devotion. When Paul used the body metaphor, he emphasized the need for every member to participate in the church, but when he used the family metaphor, he was illustrating the emotional aspects of relational Christianity.

God designed the church, the family of God, to be a "reparenting organism" to bring emotional and spiritual healing to people who have grown up in unhealthy families. Many people today need to learn for the first time how to love and care for others. They may have never experienced this kind of environment before. When the church functions as God says it should, these believers see it modeled in their new, extended family.

Honor One Another

"Honor one another above yourselves" (Rom. 12:10).

Jesus Christ gave us the supreme example of how to honor others above ourselves. Shortly before His death He taught the disciples a powerful truth. At an evening meal together, Jesus—knowing full well "that the Father had put all things under his power, and that he had come from God and was returning to God" (John 13:3)—filled a basin with water and stooped to wash His disciples' feet. After He had finished the task, He shared with them a lesson they undoubtedly never forgot.

"Do you understand," He asked, "what I have done for you?" Then He answered His own question. "You call Me 'Teacher' and 'Lord,' and rightly so, for that is what I am. Now that I, your Lord and Teacher, have washed your feet, you also should wash one another's feet. I have set you an example that you should do as I have done for you" (13:12–15).

On an earlier occasion Jesus spelled out the same truth of humility, as He took the religious leaders to task for their pride and arrogance. "Everything they do is done for men to see," He said. "They love the place of honor at banquets and the most important seats in the synagogues; they love to be greeted in the marketplaces and to have men call them 'Rabbi'" (Matt. 23:5–7). Then Jesus turned to His disciples and drove home the lesson they had to learn if they were to be mature men of God who could be used in His service: "The greatest among you will be your servant. For whoever exalts himself will be humbled, and whoever humbles himself will be exalted" (23:11–12).

The apostle Paul, though he never sat at the feet of Christ while He taught on earth, learned to honor others. He applied this truth in his own life, and he taught others to do the same. As he wrote to the Philippians, "Your attitude should be the same as that of Christ Jesus" (Phil. 2:5).

What was that attitude? Paul carefully spelled it out. Christ demonstrated toward all humankind the greatest unselfishness, humility, and self-sacrifice ever known in the universe. "Who, being in very nature God, did not consider equality with God something to be grasped, but made himself nothing, taking the very nature of a servant, being made in human likeness. And being found in appearance as a man, he humbled himself and became obedient to death—even death on a cross!" (2:6–8).

To make sure the Philippians understood what he meant by imitating Christ's attitudes and actions, he introduced this paragraph about Christ's act of humility and unselfishness by these words: "Do nothing out of selfish ambition or vain conceit, but in humility consider others better than yourselves. Each of you should look not only to your own interests, but also to the interests of others" (2:3–4).

Of course, the Bible doesn't teach that we should not have our own interests. That would be impossible. The very nature of life—making a living, rearing a family, competing in the workplace, taking time for ourselves—demands that we look after our own interests. However, the Bible teaches, as Paul wrote, that we should "look *not only*" to our "own interests, but also to the interests of others." We should "consider others better than ourselves." We should not be motivated by self-centered motives and pride ("vain conceit"). Our goal should be to honor Jesus Christ first, others second, and ourselves third. If we do, we will be honored in due time. As Jesus said, we cannot lose our lives without finding them again (Matt. 10:39).

Be of the Same Mind with One Another

"Now may the God who gives perseverance and encouragement grant you to be of the same mind with one another according to Christ Jesus" (Rom. 15:5, NASB).

Paul's prayer for unity among Christians is basically the same as Jesus' prayer recorded in John 17. In His prayer the Lord referred to at least four major elements in the incomparable message of Christianity—salvation (17:1–3), the Incarnation (17:4–6), sanctification (17:17–19), and glorification (17:24). Central to this beautiful and profound prayer is one major request—that Christ's disciples (and Christians everywhere) might experience unity and oneness. "Holy Father," prayed Jesus, "protect them by the power of your name—the name you gave me—so that they may be one as we are one" (17:11).

Later in the same prayer Jesus amplified this request: "My prayer is not for them alone. I pray also for those who will believe in me through their message [all believers], that all of them may be one, Father, just as you are in me and I am in you. May they also be in us so that the world may believe that you have sent me. I have given them the glory that you gave me, that they may be one as we are one; I in them and you in me. May they be brought to complete unity to let the world know that you sent me and have loved them even as you have loved me" (17:20–23).

One of Satan's primary strategies throughout church history has been to destroy unity among Bible-believing Christians and thereby drive people away from Christ. But this is also why Satan has tried to create a sense of unity among false religions—particularly those that deny the deity of Christ.

What an incredible twofold strategy! On the one hand, Satan tries to destroy love and unity in the churches that truly believe in the deity of Jesus Christ. On the other hand, he attempts to simulate love and unity in churches and groups that deny the deity of Christ. Unfortunately people are repulsed by disunity among those people who have the truth, and they are attracted to groups that simulate unity even though they don't believe the truth.

Thankfully God gave us a strategy for defeating Satan. When we follow the "one-another" admonitions in Scripture by walking in the Spirit, we will be "of the same mind with one another."

Accept One Another

"Accept one another, then, just as Christ accepted you, in order to bring praise to God" (Rom. 15:7).

We are to accept other Christians just as Jesus Christ accepted us. But how did He receive us? Did He say, "I will accept you if you speak German"? (Incidentally, at one time, this was a part of the division and disunity in the church in which I grew up. In fact, that whole church was permeated with German culture, which was often equated with biblical Christianity.)

Obviously Jesus does not accept or reject people because they do or do not speak a certain language. Neither does Jesus accept people into His family based on their skin color, race, status, wealth, age, or gender. When a person becomes a Christian, Jesus Christ accepts that individual unconditionally. "It is by grace" we "have been saved, through faith." Salvation "is the gift of God," and we do not receive it "by works, so that no one can boast" (Eph. 2:8–9).

Jesus Christ doesn't even ask us to "clean up our act" before He accepts us. Rather, He has said that He accepts us just as we are—weaknesses and all. He tells us to come to Him and receive Him and *He* will "clean up our act." This is what Paul meant after his great declaration that salvation is by grace through faith: "For we are God's workmanship, created in Christ Jesus to do good works, which God prepared in advance for us to do" (2:10).

Paul also stated that *showing partiality* is a barrier to unity and acceptance of others. "Live in harmony with one another," he wrote. "Don't be proud, but be willing to associate with people of low position. Don't be conceited" (Rom. 12:16).

James called this sin "prejudice." He allowed no room for misinterpretation when he wrote, "As believers in our glorious Lord Jesus Christ, don't show favoritism" (James 2:1). James was addressing a particular problem involving the rich and the poor. When a rich, well-dressed man came into their assembly, the leaders immediately gave him the best seat. But when a poor, shabbily clothed man came in, they ushered him to a less prominent seat. When you do this, James asked, "Have you not discriminated among yourselves and become judges of evil thoughts?" (2:4). To make sure they got his point, James answered to his own question in unequivocal terms: "If you show favoritism, you sin" (2:9).

Prejudice, favoritism, and discrimination in the body of Christ lead to the rejection and alienation of some Christians. This violates God's standards. Furthermore, this kind of behavior violates the very nature of the body of Christ. We are all one. Every member is important—rich or poor, young or old, black and white, weak or strong, Swedish or Slavic, those who speak English and those who speak Spanish or any other language. If we show favoritism, we destroy the unity, harmony, and oneness in the body of Christ which Christ and Paul both prayed for and commanded. We are to "accept one another" just as Christ accepted us.

Admonish One Another

"And concerning you, my brethren, I myself also am convinced that you yourselves are full of goodness, filled with all knowledge, and able also to admonish one another" (Rom. 15:14, NASB).

Translators use various words to describe Paul's injunction here to the Roman Christians. The Greek word *noutheteō* is rendered "admonish" (NASB, NKJV) "counsel" (Williams), and "instruct" (NIV).

Noutheteō doesn't refer to casual communication or normal teaching and counseling. It implies a definite exhortation, a correction. The New International Version renders this verb by the word "warn" in 1 Thessalonians 5:14, in which Paul admonished Christians not to be idle and lazy. This word is also translated "warn" in Acts 20:31 and 1 Corinthians 4:14.

Paul's exhortation to "admonish one another" (Rom. 15:14) is a divine balance to his instruction to "accept one another." Of course, we are not to "accept" a person's sinful behavior. We can accept a sinner without accepting his or her sin. In fact, it's our unconditional acceptance of others that gives us credibility to admonish and correct. By accepting others as Christ accepted us, we earn the right to admonish others who are straying from the path God has outlined for us in the Scriptures.

Paul complimented the Roman Christians by letting them know he was convinced that they were "competent to instruct [admonish] one another." What makes a believer competent to admonish others? Paul wrote that the Christians in Rome were qualified to admonish others because of two things in their own lives: They were "full of goodness" and they were "complete in knowledge" (15:14). These believers were able to admonish other believers because they were making progress in their own Christian lives. Though they weren't perfect, they were mature enough to make sure they had removed the "plank" from their own eyes before they tried to remove the "speck of sawdust" from a brother's eye (Matt. 7:3–5).

Christians who are sensitive about their own walk with God are capable—and responsible—to admonish other Christians. They have earned the right to warn those who display characteristics that violate the direct teaching of Scripture. Putting it another way, we must make sure we clean up our own act before we try to help others clean up theirs.

Also we can admonish others if we, like the Romans, have an adequate knowledge of God's Word. Admonishing must be based on God's specific will and ways—not on what we think other Christians should or should not be doing. We must be careful at this point. Many Christians tend to confuse absolutes and nonabsolutes. If we exhort Christians in areas that are extrabiblical—areas that are not specifically spelled out in Scripture or things that involve cultural standards and practices—then we are in danger of imposing standards contrary to Scripture.

The Bible gives us some additional guidelines on how to admonish: with deep concern and love (Acts 20:31), from pure motives (1 Cor. 4:14), with the proper goal in mind (Col. 1:28–29), and in spiritual wisdom (3:16).

Greet One Another

"Greet Priscilla and Aquila. . . . Greet also the church that meets at their house. Greet my dear friend Epenetus. . . . Greet Mary, who worked very hard for you. . . . Greet one another with a holy kiss. All the churches of Christ send greetings" (Rom. 16:3–6, 16).

When Paul closed his Roman letter, he extended a whole series of "greetings" to various people who meant a lot to him. He mentioned twenty-six people by name. Being called by one's name means much to everyone. This social grace takes discipline, especially when we are meeting many new people all the time.

After Paul mentioned these people by name and greeted them directly and indirectly with some special words of commendation and appreciation, he told them to "greet one another with a holy kiss" (16:16). This injunction is given four other times in the New Testament (1 Cor. 16:20; 2 Cor. 13:12; 1 Thess. 5:26; 1 Pet. 5:14).

In some respects this "one another" exhortation differs from the others. All the injunctions we've looked at so far focus on function. However, to greet one another with a holy kiss includes both function and form. On the one hand, to "greet one another" is a function that is normative. We are to do this in every cultural situation. However, the "form" of that greeting will vary. Put another way, as Christians, we're always to greet each other sincerely as brothers and sisters in Christ. However, the way that greeting is expressed depends on what is appropriate and expected in a given culture.

Thus, as discussed earlier, forms vary from culture to culture. And yet, regardless of the forms these functions take in the Christian community, they should never violate biblical values. Paul's concern was not the form of the greeting, but rather that it be a "holy" (sanctified) greeting, an expression of true Christian love. It is to demonstrate that believers are truly brothers and sisters in Christ. It is not to be just a greeting, a routine gesture that reflects the social graces of a particular culture. It is to be sincere and meaningful, reflecting God's care and concern for us all.

Mature Christians can and should show physical affection. In our society, shaking hands, a kiss on the cheek, and a hearty embrace are certainly appropriate. Most Christians can express this kind of affection. But it must always be based on pure motives, discretion, and above all, true Christian love. When it is expressed inappropriately, reflecting impure motives, indiscretion, and selfish actions, it can lead to hurt, bitterness, and even immorality. But expressed properly it can help foster oneness, unity, and even spiritual and psychological healing.

SUMMARY

As believers follow the many New Testament "one another" injunctions, they manifest the fruit of the Spirit. In addition they demonstrate the unity and spiritual growth that God desires for His people. Like a human body, with its parts "joined and held together by every supporting ligament," the church, the body of Christ, grows "in love, as each part does its work" (Eph. 4:16). *This is the key to growth—both spiritually and numerically.*

6

Foundations for Evangelism and Missions

THROUGHOUT THESE CHAPTERS, we've emphasized that faith, hope, and love—especially love—are the true marks of a mature church. In this chapter, we'll see why love is "the greatest of these" (1 Cor. 13:13). *Love, we believe, is the most important key to church growth.*

THE UPPER ROOM EXPERIENCE

In the Upper Room Jesus spoke of the importance of love as the basis for reaching people for Christ. "A new command I give to you: Love one another. As I have loved you, so you must love one another. By this all men will know that you are my disciples, if you love one another" (John 13:34–35).

When Jesus told these eleven men about this new commandment—to "love one another"—they, of course, were well aware of the "old commandment," or more accurately, the "old commandments" (plural). Jesus contrasted the "new commandment" with the Law of Moses as embodied in the Ten Commandments given by God at Mount Sinai.

On earlier occasions Jesus had already summarized the Law by referring to "love." For example, one day when Jesus was teaching in Jerusalem, a religious leader—a scribe—approached Him and asked, "Of all the commandments, which is the most important?" Jesus responded, "The most important one . . . is this: 'Hear, O Israel, the Lord our God, the Lord is one. Love the Lord your God with all your heart and with all your soul and with all your mind and with all your strength.' The second is this:

'Love your neighbor as yourself.' There is no commandment greater than these" (Mark 12:28–31).

As Jesus prepared His disciples that day in the Upper Room for His death and resurrection, He also prepared them for their mission in the world. All along Jesus had emphasized the need for these men to put God first in their lives. However, in the Upper Room Jesus focused on the horizontal or relational dimension of love—to "love one another." Jesus said what Paul later explained in his letter to the Romans, namely, that all the commands given at Mount Sinai that deal with human relationships are summarized in one commandment, the commandment to love others: "Let no debt remain outstanding, except the continuing debt to love one another, for he who loves his fellowman has fulfilled the law. The commandments, 'Do not commit adultery,' 'Do not murder,' 'Do not steal,' 'Do not covet,' and whatever other commandment there may be, are summed up in this one rule: 'Love your neighbor as yourself.' Love does no harm to its neighbor. Therefore love is the fulfillment of the law" (Rom. 13:8–10).

Christ's Unusual Example

When Jesus gave His disciples this new command to love each other, He did not ask them to do something He was not willing to do Himself. In fact, John began this chapter with the words, "Jesus knew that the time had come for him to leave this world and go to the Father. Having loved his own who were in the world, he now showed them the full extent of his love" (John 13:1).

The "full extent of his love" was Christ's willingness to die on the cross for the apostles' sins and for the sins of the whole world (3:16). However, these men in no way were prepared at this moment in their lives to understand that Christ was to die for them. Though He had told them it would happen, they could not understand it, believe it, or accept it. Therefore Jesus prepared them step-by-step to understand what real love is all about.

Jesus Became the Servant

Jesus illustrated this love by washing their feet. When they arrived in that Upper Room, the meal was prepared. Everything was in place. In fact, there was a basin of water and a towel available. However, one important person was missing. There was no servant to wash their feet when they arrived. It was customary in those days for a servant to wash the feet of the guests before a meal. They had been walking through the dirty, dusty streets of Jerusalem—either barefoot or with sandals.

Significantly, when they arrived in the room, with the servant missing, not one of these men volunteered to be the servant. They knew what was customary—and necessary. They were simply unwilling to serve one another.

I believe that Jesus purposely waited to give one of them an opportunity to become "the servant" before He made His move. He "got up from the meal, took off his outer clothing, and wrapped a towel around his waist." He then "poured water into a basin and began to wash his disciples' feet, drying them with the towel that was wrapped around him" (John 13:4–5).

Peter's Embarrassment

When Simon Peter's turn came, he resisted Jesus. This may be because Peter was ashamed, which may explain his extreme reactions (John 13:8–9). He no doubt sensed Jesus' reason for His actions, since the apostle had not volunteered to be the servant, even though he should have. To his credit, he at least revealed his own embarrassment by initially not allowing Christ to wash his feet.

A Powerful Lesson

When Jesus completed this act of love, He made His point. He began with a question: "Do you understand what I have done for you? . . . You call me 'Teacher' and 'Lord,' and rightly so, for that is what I am. Now that I, your Lord and Teacher, have washed your feet, you also should wash one another's feet. I have set you an example that you should do as I have done for you" (John 13:12–15).

In many respects this was a shocking experience for the disciples. It threatened them, especially in view of their prideful arguments among themselves as to who was to be the greatest. It hit at the very heart of their self-centeredness, their desire to dominate and control one another. As Merrill Tenney commented, "They were ready to fight for a throne, but not for a towel!"[1]

Christ's Ultimate Purpose

Jesus had a far greater purpose in washing the disciples' feet than simply teaching them to serve each other. "By this," He said, "all men will know that you are my disciples, if you love one another" (John 13:35).

There were many disciples in Jesus' day—disciples of Moses, disciples of the Pharisees, and disciples of John the Baptist. A disciple was a learner, a follower of a teacher or leader. Jesus wanted everyone to know that these eleven men were *His* disciples, and this would be known by their love for each other. Later these same disciples were called Christians because they were followers of Christ (Acts 11:26). They exemplified His life.

THE VINEYARD EXPERIENCE

As Jesus and the disciples left the Upper Room, they made their way to the outskirts of Jerusalem (John 14:31). While they were walking along, Jesus again underscored the fact that He wanted them to make Him known to others. As they walked by a vineyard He said, "This is to my Father's glory, that you bear much fruit, showing yourselves to be my disciples" (15:8).

During the Passover meal Jesus had used the foot-washing incident to help the disciples understand the meaning of His love and how they should demonstrate that love to one another. This time Jesus told about a vine and its branches to make a spiritual point.

Jesus may have passed an actual vineyard on the edge of Jerusalem. Perhaps He pointed to freshly pruned branches in the vineyard as He said, "I am the true vine, and my Father is the gardener. He cuts off every branch in me that bears no fruit, while every branch that does bear fruit he prunes so that it will be even more fruitful" (15:1–2).

Judas, though he had appeared to be a fruit-bearing branch, had already left the group and was making final plans to betray Christ. His tragic destiny lay just ahead, but the eleven men who remained belonged to Christ.

In this illustration Christ stated that the vinedresser or gardener is His Father (15:1), and that He, Jesus, is the true Vine. Obviously the freshly pruned branches represented the eleven disciples who had not forsaken Him (15:2–3). However, Christ did not initially and directly define the word *fruit* as He did the other aspects of this allegory.

What did Christ actually mean? When we compare the statement Jesus made in the Upper Room ("By this all men will know that you are my disciples, if you love one another," 13:35) with the statement He made about the vineyard ("This is to my Father's glory, that you bear much fruit, showing yourselves to be my disciples," 15:8), the similarity is obvious.

Since Jesus made both of these statements as He was preparing His disciples for His death and resurrection, it is logical to conclude that the fruit referred to in John 15 includes their love for one another. This is verified by the next statements He made: "As the Father has loved me, so have I loved you. Now remain in my love. If you obey my commands, you will remain in my love, just as I have obeyed my Father's commands and remain in his love. . . . My command is this: Love each other as I have loved you. Greater love has no one than this, that he lay down his life for his friends. . . . This is my command: Love each other" (15:9–10, 12–13, 17).

A Deeper Dimension of Love

When we read in Scripture that we are to "love one another," we often think of ways by which we can demonstrate kindness, patience, and unselfishness, as defined in 1 Corinthians 13. However, even in this classic love chapter, love has a deeper dimension. It includes the way we treat each other at a moral and ethical level. In this sense it also involves righteousness, holiness, and purity in our relationships.

Paul developed this dimension of love in his letter to the Philippian Christians, particularly in his prayer for them in Philippians 1:9–11. "And this is my prayer: that your love may abound more and more in knowledge and depth of insight, so that you may be able to discern what is best and may be pure and blameless until the day of Christ, filled with the fruit of righteousness that comes through Jesus Christ—to the glory and praise of God." Paul's words in Ephesians 5:8–9 also emphasize this dimension of love: "For you were once darkness, but now you are light in the Lord. Live as children of light (for the fruit of the light consists in all goodness, righteousness and truth)."

JESUS' PRAYER FOR UNITY

The next major event in this unique sequence of events involved Jesus' prayer as He and His eleven disciples were heading toward the Kidron Valley. As Jesus looked toward heaven, He prayed, "Father, the time has come. Glorify your Son, that your Son may glorify you. For you granted him authority over all people that he might give eternal life to all those you have given him. Now this is eternal life: that they may know you, the only true God, and Jesus Christ, whom you have sent" (John 17:1–3).

Later in Jesus' prayer He specified His divine plan for convincing people that He had come from God. He prayed not only for His disciples, but also for Christians all over the world who would come to know Him down through the centuries. "My prayer is not for them alone. I pray also for those who will believe in me through their message, that all of them may be one, Father, just as you are in me and I am in you. May they also be in us so that the world may believe that you have sent me. I have given them the glory that you gave me, that they may be one as we are one: I in them and you in me. May they be brought to complete unity to let the world know that you sent me and have loved them even as you have loved me" (17:20–23).

Jesus' statements in the Upper Room, plus His comments as He referred to the vine and the branches and then His words in this prayer, together form one of the greatest missionary and evangelistic statements of all time. Before Jesus told these men to go and make disciples (Matt. 28:19), He wanted the world to know what dedicated disciples of Jesus Christ are like. In essence, they are to reflect their commitment to Him through their love for one another and the unity and oneness this love produces.

THE JERUSALEM MODEL

This is why the Jerusalem model is such a powerful example (see chapter 4). We see in this church what Jesus had taught the apostles before His death and resurrection. As the unsaved people in Jerusalem observed these believers devoting themselves to "the apostles' teaching and to the fellowship, to the breaking of bread and to prayer"; as unbelievers saw those following Christ selling all they possessed and sharing the proceeds with all those in need; as they saw the disciples continuing every day to meet together in the temple courts, eating together "with glad and sincere hearts, praising God;" as they observed the believers' love for each other—these believers had the "favor of all the people." The result was that "the Lord added to their number daily those who were being saved" (Acts 2:42–47).

This dynamic love and oneness that was demonstrated among the Jerusalem Christians became the bridge to the unsaved world. It provided a basis for demonstrating that Jesus Christ is indeed who He said He is—God in the flesh who had come with one purpose, to seek and to save those who are lost (Luke 19:10). Along with the apostles these Christians carried out Jesus' new commandment given in the Upper Room. They were "bearing fruit" in all their relationships, thus demonstrating their abiding relationship with Jesus Christ. Furthermore, what we see in Jerusalem is a dramatic answer to Jesus' prayer in John 17. Those who were added to the church daily truly believed that Jesus Christ is the Messiah, the Son of God.

GOD'S PLAN IN PERSPECTIVE

To understand more fully God's unique evangelistic and mission strategy for building a bridge to the world through the local church, let's look at a series of questions and answers, particularly as they relate to why John wrote his Gospel in the first place.

Why Did Jesus Christ Come into This World?

Jesus answered that question in His discourse about Himself as the Good Shepherd. "I have come that they may have life, and have it to the full. I am the good shepherd. The good shepherd lays down his life for the sheep"

(John 10:10–11). In His discourse on Himself as the Bread of Life, He said, "I am the living bread that came down from heaven. If anyone eats of this bread, he will live forever. This bread is my flesh, which I will give for the life of the world" (6:51).

Speaking to Martha, after her brother Lazarus had died, Jesus said, "I am the resurrection and the life. He who believes in me will live, even though he dies; and whoever lives and believes in me will never die. Do you believe this?" (11:25–26). And speaking to doubters in Jerusalem, He said, "I have come into the world as a light, so that no one who believes in me should stay in darkness" (12:46).

John wrote his Gospel to tell his readers that Jesus came into this world for one purpose—to give eternal life to all who trust Him.

Why Was Jesus Christ Able to Be Our Savior from Sin?

As Jesus spoke to the Jewish leaders of His day, He left no question in their minds about who He claimed to be: "'Your father Abraham rejoiced at the thought of seeing my day; he saw it and was glad.' 'You are not yet fifty years old,' the Jews said to him, 'and you have seen Abraham!' 'I tell you the truth,' Jesus answered, 'before Abraham was born, I am!'" (John 8:56–58). The Pharisees then knew exactly who Jesus claimed to be. When He said "I am," they would have immediately thought of the time when Moses, afraid to return to Egypt, was reassured by God that He, the "I AM," had sent him (Exod. 3:14).

Later when the Jews asked Him to tell them plainly who He is, He said, "I and the Father are one" (John 10:30). John made it clear that because He was God in the flesh, God incarnate, Jesus Christ could be our Savior.

How Did Christ Verify That He Is Indeed One with God the Father?

Christ did not rely on words alone to convince people that He is the Son of God and the Savior of the world. He demonstrated His deity and verified His words with miraculous signs. In fact, one of the major purposes John had in mind in writing his Gospel was to demonstrate Christ's deity by selecting and recording some of His unique miracles. John stated this purpose in John 20:30–31.

John recorded seven of Jesus' pre-Cross miracles, uniquely designed to cause people to believe that He is God. Merrill Tenney points out that each miracle demonstrates a unique aspect of Christ's deity.[1]

- When Jesus changed the water into wine, the best wine on that occasion, He demonstrated that He is the Master of *quality* (2:1–11).
- When Jesus healed the nobleman's son, while the boy was more than twenty miles away, He showed He is the Master of *distance* or *space* (4:43–54).
- When Jesus instantaneously healed the impotent man who had been crippled for thirty-eight years, He demonstrated that He is the Master of *time* (5:1–14).
- When Jesus miraculously fed the five thousand (besides women and children), He demonstrated He is the Master of *quantity* (6:1–14).
- When Jesus walked on the water, He demonstrated He is the Master of *the physical world* (6:16–21).
- When Jesus healed the man who had been born blind, He demonstrated He is the Master over *misfortune* (9:1–38).
- When Jesus raised Lazarus from the dead, He demonstrated He is the Master over *death* (11:1–44).

Each of these seven miracle-signs points dramatically to the fact that Jesus Christ is who He claimed to be—God in the flesh. This is why John began his Gospel by coming right to the point as he did in John 1:1–3, 14.

What Is God's Plan Today for Demonstrating That Jesus Christ Is God in the Flesh?

As we have observed, Jesus claimed to be God and demonstrated that fact with a number of miracles. But in His high-priestly prayer in John 17 He asked for a new kind of miracle-sign to demonstrate to the world that He is from God—the miracle of love that is manifested in oneness and unity among His followers. He would no longer be visibly present to demonstrate His deity, as He had been for three and a half years. But He left behind a small group of men, who through their love and unity would demonstrate their relationship to Jesus Christ. Throughout the centuries God's plan is that Christians everywhere emulate Christ. Francis Schaeffer has called this unity "the final apologetic."[2]

No amount of intellectual arguing to prove the deity of Christ can replace the reality of Christianity flowing through Christians who are in a proper relationship with one another. Interestingly Christians are to judge whether others are true followers of Christ by what they believe— their doctrine (1 John 2:20–23). Anyone who says Jesus Christ is not from God can't be classified as a true believer. But the world is to judge Christianity by the way Christians live—their love and their fruit—which reflects itself in unity and oneness. In this dynamic context the Holy Spirit releases His miraculous power to convince unbelievers that Christ is one with God and the Savior of the world.

What Has Been Satan's Strategic Plan from the First Century until the Present Time?

We know that Satan has always had a two-pronged attack. On the one hand, he attempts to get people who deny the deity of Christ to simulate love and unity. And on the other hand, he attempts to destroy love and unity among those who believe that Jesus Christ is the Son of God.

Satan's tactic to simulate love and unity. We can see this demonstrated most readily in various cults. Many non-Christians and even immature Christians are attracted to these religious systems because they often demonstrate more concern and love than people in Bible-believing churches. This, of course, is a tragedy since Christians, of all people, should be demonstrating the love Jesus commanded and the unity He prayed for.

Satan's tactic to destroy love and unity. Satan's second tactic is to destroy love and unity in churches that truly believe in the deity of Jesus Christ. It would be startling and disturbing to know for sure how many people have left churches that teach right doctrine to join various cults— primarily because they were disillusioned with Christians who did not "walk their talk."

Disunity among Christians is one of the worst forms of ugliness and repulsion, whereas true love and unity in Christ are attractive and beautiful. They provide the backdrop against which we can share the message of salvation. And strange as it may seem, this too is a miracle of God's power. In some respects this convinces people that Jesus Christ is the Son of God. How sad that some non-Christian groups demonstrate more love and unity than true Christians!

Thankfully, this need not happen. Satan need not be victorious, because Christ *prayed* for us! Furthermore, we have His Word, which exhorts us to endeavor "to keep the unity of the Spirit through the bond of peace" (Eph. 4:3). And the Holy Spirit, who indwells each believer, can release God's power to defeat Satan (3:16–21; 6:10–18).

MAKING THE INVISIBLE GOD VISIBLE TODAY

The great salvation provided by Christ "was confirmed to us by those who heard him"—obviously the apostles. And "God also testified to it"— both the message taught by Jesus and the apostles—"by signs, wonders and various miracles, and gifts of the Holy Spirit distributed according to his will" (Heb. 2:3–4).

However, how could this message be verified after Jesus Christ returned to heaven? How could the message of salvation through Christ be demonstrated after the apostles—the primary recipients of these special gifts of power—passed off the scene? I believe John gives us the answer in 1 John 4:11–12: "Dear friends, since God so loved us, we also ought to love one another. No one has ever seen God; but if we love one another, God lives in us and his love is made complete in us."

Here John described the miracle of love and unity. If believers in a local church love each other as Christ loved them, God in Christ is "fleshed out" in these people. When this happens, we demonstrate that Jesus Christ was indeed God in the flesh. The invisible God becomes visible when Christ is incarnate in a body of loving, unified believers.

This was what was happening in Jerusalem. This is why the believers had favor with all the people. The true Source of the message of eternal life was sensed, felt, accepted, and believed! Today churches that reflect true Christlike love will indeed grow spiritually and numerically. Like the Jerusalem church in its initial days, the Lord will be adding to our number daily those who are being saved (Acts 2:47). *Christian love and unity are the two essential ingredients in church growth that we often overlook!*

7

God's Plan for Church Leadership

LEADERSHIP IS AN ESSENTIAL CONSIDERATION in church planting and growth. When we have the right people in the right positions—people who are qualified in character and who have a biblical philosophy of ministry—churches will grow not only numerically but also spiritually.

Paul and Barnabas illustrated this process in a specific way on their first missionary journey.

- First, while they were in Derbe, "they preached the good news in that city and won [or made] a large number of disciples" (Acts 14:21)
- Second, they returned to Lystra, Iconium, and Antioch, cities where they had already made disciples, "strengthening the disciples and encouraging them to remain true to the faith" (14:22). The Greek word for "strengthen" is *episterizō*, "to support, reestablish, confirm," and the word for "encourage" is *parakaleō*, "to comfort, exhort, implore."

AN ADDED DIMENSION

Luke then recorded an additional dimension to this process of evangelism and edification. When local churches were established in the first century, spiritual leaders were appointed to lead these churches. Paul and Barnabas also "appointed elders for them in each church and, with prayer and fasting, committed them to the Lord, in whom they had put their trust" (Acts 14:23).

This is the first reference to the appointment of local-church leaders, although Luke referred to "apostles and elders" who were already in the Jerusalem church (15:4, 6, 22–23). We can assume that at some point in the early years of this church, the apostles appointed elders. James, the Lord's brother, seems to have been the leader of the elders (15:13), while Peter was the leader of the apostles (15:6). The church in Jerusalem served as a home base for both groups of men. The apostles had a ministry at large in carrying out the Great Commission, and the elders had the responsibility of managing and/or shepherding the flock in Jerusalem.

We're not told how these men prepared for this leadership role. On their first missionary journey Paul and Barnabas probably looked for God-fearing Jews (like Barnabas, Stephen, and Philip) or God-fearing Gentiles (like Cornelius). Timothy was a God-fearing young man whose father was a Gentile, and who, because of his godly Jewish mother, had learned the Old Testament Scriptures from the time he was a small boy (2 Tim. 3:14–15). Obviously when men like this were converted to Jesus Christ, they matured quickly. Their knowledge of the Old Testament suddenly took on new meaning once they understood that Jesus Christ is the true Messiah. Because they were strong spiritual leaders in the Jewish community before they became Christians, they quickly became strong leaders in the church.

Paul also recognized the need to prepare men to be qualified leaders. This is clear from his instructions to Timothy: "And the things you have heard me say in the presence of many witnesses entrust to reliable men who will also be qualified to teach others" (2:2).

Additional Observations

Several other observations about local-church leadership can be made from the New Testament.

First, these local-church leaders are identified in Scripture with two primary titles. The word *elder (presbuteros)* was used of the leaders in the churches that were primarily populated with Jewish believers. The word *bishop* or *overseer (episkopos)* was used of spiritual leaders in churches that were populated primarily by Gentile converts. The term *elder* comes directly from the Jewish community, going as far back as the time of Moses. "The word *episkopos* is fairly common in Greek literature, papyri, and inscriptions, both in its general meaning of oversight and as a technical term for officials, civil and religious."[1] In Athens governors of conquered states were called overseers.[2]

Paul used these two terms interchangeably. Borrowed from particular cultures, one religious and one secular, they were given new meanings and new functions within the Christian culture. We see here, then, a cultural adaptation in the use of language in order to communicate more effectively. This cultural adaptation explains why the term *bishop* was never used to describe the local-church leaders in Jerusalem; they were called "elders" because they were Jews. This also explains why the term *elder* and *bishop* are used interchangeably in association with the churches in Ephesus, Philippi, and Crete (Acts 20:17, 28; 1 Tim. 3:1–2; 5:17, 19; Titus 1:5–7). These three geographical areas were heavily populated by *both* Jews and Gentiles.

Second, these local-church spiritual leaders were to manage and/or shepherd God's people. Two words that describe the responsibilities of elders are *managing* and *pastoring* or *shepherding.* Managing is the more technical term, whereas pastoring and shepherding are more colorful and illustrative concepts.

Managing a Church

Paul first used the word *manage* in his writings when listing the qualifications for elders. An elder, he wrote, "must be one who manages his own household well" (1 Tim. 3:4, NASB). Paul correlated this observation with leadership in a local church: "If anyone does not know how to manage his own family, how can he take care of God's church?" (3:5).

This is an important observation. It demonstrates a relationship in Paul's thinking between a family unit and the local church. A single household was often a "church in miniature." The father was to lead his family just as elders were to lead the church. In fact, in some instances the father was probably *both* father and elder. This seems to be true of a man like Philemon.

Paul's illustration gives us a functional definition of the word *manage*. It is an all-inclusive concept. There is nothing that is not included in this task. It involved total and complete oversight of the family—or the church. Put another way, God holds the father responsible for overall leadership in the home, and He holds elders responsible for overall leadership in the local church.

Pastoring a Flock

The Greek word *poimainō*, "to pastor or shepherd," is used more frequently in Scripture to describe the overall leadership responsibility of an elder than the words *manage* or *rule*. This concept would be meaningful to first-century Christians, who understood the relationship between a shepherd and his sheep.

Peter exhorted elders to shepherd "God's flock." They were to do it with freedom (not under compulsion) and with true motives (not for money). Nor were they to approach this task in an authoritarian manner, lording it over those allotted to them. Rather, they were to be "examples to the flock" (1 Pet. 5:1–3).

Just as a shepherd is responsible for the total welfare of his sheep, so a pastor is to care for his people. He is to guard them from "savage wolves," that is, false teachers (Acts 20:28–29). He is to feed them by declaring and teaching the "whole purpose of God" (20:27, NASB; see also Titus 1:9).

Managing and shepherding, then, are overarching concepts that include specific functions such as exemplifying Christlikeness, preaching the gospel, exhorting and warning Christians against inappropriate behavior, and teaching the truth of God.

Third, some of these leaders were to be remunerated for their ministry. Paul wrote that "the elders who rule well be considered worthy of double honor, especially those who work hard at preaching and teaching" (1 Tim. 5:17, NASB). Paul followed this exhortation with two quotations from the Old Testament: "For the Scripture says, 'Do not muzzle the ox while it is treading out the grain,' and 'The worker deserves his wages'" (5:18).

This is the biblical basis for identifying some spiritual leaders as staff elders and/or pastors. When an individual gives a large portion of time to the ministry, that person usually doesn't have time to work at a regular job in order to provide for his family. If a body of believers encourages and accepts this kind of effort, then they are responsible to remunerate that person for his efforts.

This verse of Scripture is used by some to establish two kinds of elders—"ruling elders" and "teaching elders." However, Paul may have been simply saying that some of the elders who carry out their ruling or managing role will be particularly involved in preaching and teaching. Those of us who serve as staff pastors can certainly verify that these are (or should be) the most time-consuming aspects of managing or shepherding. In other words, all elders are "ruling elders" in the sense of being leaders, but some will spend more time than others in carrying out this function by spending a lot of time preaching and teaching—an important part of managing or pastoring the flock.

Fourth, New Testament churches evidently had more than one elder. The Bible always speaks of the "elders" of a church, that is, the term is used in the plural. The only exception is when an elder's qualifications are referred to, as in 1 Timothy 3:1–2. The word *church* often referred to all believers in a particular geographic area, whether they met together in one location or not. For example, Luke referred to the "church at Jerusalem" (Acts 8:1). But we know that as more people were saved, not all the believers in any given city were able to continue meeting in one place.

Luke referred to the "elders of the church" in Ephesus (20:17). And the same is true in Crete. Paul left Titus there to help organize new churches. He was to "appoint elders in every town" (Titus 1:5). Again the word *elder* was used in the plural, so we can conclude that Titus was to appoint more than one elder in each city.

Assuming that the churches in Crete met in homes, as they did in other places in the New Testament worlds, we can now raise some interesting questions.

- Was there one elder for every house church? If so, this would in no way contradict the previous references to the plurality of elders in Jerusalem or Ephesus. It would simply mean there was more than one house church in each city.

• Was there more than one elder in each house church? Perhaps, but probably not, unless the house church was unusually large. This is a possibility, however, since archaeologists have discovered homes used for church meetings that had large rooms and/or courtyards that could seat hundreds of people. In a large house church probably more than one elder would have been needed to manage and shepherd all the believers.

In these biblical examples we can conclude that there was more than one elder in the church in Jerusalem, the church in Ephesus, and the church in Crete. The same would be true in Lystra, Iconium, and Pisidian Antioch, since we are told that in these cities Paul and Barnabas "appointed elders for them in each church" (Acts 14:23). But we do not have sufficient biblical data about church structure to explain more fully the concept of elder plurality and how this actually worked out in given localities.

Fifth, these spiritual leaders were to delegate responsibility to other qualified men and women to care for the needs of the church. When Paul wrote to Timothy, who was stationed at the time in Ephesus, he first specified the qualifications for elders (1 Tim. 3:1–7). Then he noted the qualifications for deacons, that is, men in serving roles (3:8–10, 12). It also seems that he mentioned qualifications for deaconesses, that is, women in serving roles (3:11).

What were these people supposed to do in the church? Interestingly the biblical writers did not specify the functions of deacons and deaconesses as they did for elders. Qualifications are spelled out, but not their specific responsibilities.

The role of elders is supracultural. That is, no matter what their social background, Christians will always need to be managed, pastored, taught the Word of God, and ministered to in other spiritual ways. On the other hand, cultural needs vary from society to society, community to community, and from time to time, calling for different cultural functions by deacons and deaconesses. For example, think of the oil and real estate crisis and the Savings and Loan crisis that precipitated a serious recession a few years ago. Beginning in the southwestern United States, it soon impacted many parts of the world. This economic crisis also impacted our churches—including the church I (Gene Getz) pastor. So the elders appointed a special task force to explore what the Scriptures say about this kind of crisis and how the church should respond. We identified this group as our "Acts 6 group," modeled after the seven men who were appointed in Jerusalem to care for the needy widows (see Acts 6:1–7). Following their study and evaluation, the group proposed a plan to the elders on how to address this problem. They did a superb job, and once they completed their task, they ceased functioning in this "deacon role"—just as the seven men ceased waiting on tables in Jerusalem once cultural needs changed. This kind of process needs to be ongoing, to meet special needs that arise.

Sixth, these spiritual leaders were to be appointed on the basis of spiritual qualifications. Two passages—1 Timothy 3:2–7; Titus 1:6–9—specify elder qualifications. Each "maturity profile" for elders in these two passages is self-contained, but in essence, they are the same. Following is the profile outlined by Paul for Timothy:

Leadership Qualifications for Elders

- Above reproach (a man with a good reputation)
- Husband of one wife (maintaining moral purity)
- Temperate (exercising sobriety and clearheadedness)
- Self-controlled (controlling his emotions and words)
- Respectable (serving as a good role model)
- Hospitable (demonstrating unselfishness and generosity)
- Able to teach (communicating sensitively in a nonthreatening and nondefensive manner)
- Not addicted to wine (not being addicted to substances)
- Not violent (not abusive)
- Gentle (sensitive, loving, and kind)
- Not quarreling (nonargumentative)
- Free from the love of money (nonmaterialistic)
- Managing his household well (a good husband and father)
- Not a new convert (not a recent Christian)
- Having a good reputation with those outside the church (a good testimony to unbelivers)

Titus 1:6–9 mentions many of these and adds these qualifications: blameless, not overbearing, loving what is good, upright, holy, disciplined, and holding firmly to the truth.

Appointing qualified spiritual leaders in a local church is the most important of these six observations. A church will either succeed or fail, depending on how seriously it takes these qualifications. One unqualified leader can destroy a local church. So it is very important to develop a means for discovering, equipping, and appointing qualified people to these important leadership roles.

TWENTIETH-CENTURY FORMS AND PATTERNS

When it comes to describing how spiritual leaders (particularly elders) did their work, the writers of Scripture tell us very little. For example, elders' functions are clear, and the qualities that are to grace their lives are spelled out in detail. But, the following "form questions" are not answered in the Bible:

How old should these leaders be? Though age is a relative concept, the word *elder* suggests a person who is experienced or above average in maturity. Certain things, of course, can be learned only over a process of time. Age and experience produce wisdom in Christians who seek to follow God's will.

How should these leaders be selected? Again, the Bible does not specify any particular method for selecting elders. We know that Paul and Barnabas, who were apostles, appointed elders (Acts 14:23), and that Timothy and Titus were told to appoint elders (1 Tim. 3:1; Titus 1:5). However, the problem today is that we have no "apostles" in the sense that Paul and Barnabas were apostles, nor do we have men appointed by apostles, such as Timothy and Titus, who stayed in certain locations and helped develop churches founded on missionary journeys.

A principle, however, that emerges from Scripture can help guide us today: In a new church, elders may be appointed by an individual or individuals who are already recognized as spiritually qualified leaders, just as Timothy and Titus were.

Whatever the approach, a system of selection should be developed that discovers and appoints qualified leaders who are highly respected by the church.

How many leaders should there be in a single church? Again, the Scriptures do not specify how many elders should serve a local church. The principle of multiple leadership seems clear in the New Testament. But the specific number for a particular church is not clear—especially since we do not even know how elders in a particular "city church" carried out their functions.

Experience, however, verifies the fact that a board of elders serving a local church should be small enough to make decisions quickly and wisely, and yet large enough to benefit from the experience and maturity of a significant number of men.

How long should these leaders serve? Though the Bible does not answer this question, it does seem to imply that once a man became an elder, he could serve in that position as long as he had time to do so and remained qualified.

However, this creates some problems when churches grow in size—which they tend to do in large population centers. When the opportunity for eldership is kept open, the elder board may grow so large that it can't function efficiently. On the other hand, when a "closed" elder system is adopted to keep the board small, the board may become "ingrown" and opportunities for other men in the church to serve as elders become limited.

One way to resolve this problem is to keep the elder board open-ended, but to have a smaller group of elders selected to serve as a decision-making group. Another approach is to have a rotating system. Some churches have elders serve on the board for three years, with one-third of the men rotating off the board each year. After one year's absence, a man can serve as an elder for another three years.

What is the best way for these leaders to carry out their functions? Since the Scriptures do not answer this question, a plan should be developed in any given culture to allow elders to carry out their functions effectively as pastors. If this is not done, these men will become only administrators, and some decisions may be made that are out of touch with people's needs.

When there is more than one spiritual elder, who takes primary leadership? It has already been pointed out that the Bible teaches multiple leadership. In fact, the more godly leaders we have in a local church, the greater will be the spiritual impact on the members at large. A core of mature elders and pastors can serve as models of Christlikeness.

Some churches have interpreted the emphasis on multiple leadership in the New Testament to mean that a church should be led by a "committee" of men with no one designated as a primary leader. One reason this idea has emerged is that churches may be overreacting to pastors who have authoritarian personalities, seeking to be in absolute control. These pastors view elders and deacons as mere figureheads doing their bidding.

It is true that we do not have scriptural examples for our present practice of appointing senior pastors, associates, assistants, and others. But neither do we have New Testament examples of a committee of men leading a church with no one designated as primary leader.

Biblical evidence points to the fact that lines of authority need to be established for effective church life to take place. For example, Paul was recognized as having authority over Timothy and Titus and other men who helped establish churches. In turn, Timothy and Titus were recognized as having authority in given cities to appoint elders. It is only logical that certain elders were given authority to give direction to the ministry in certain locations. In fact, as already noted, by the second century, the term *bishop* came to refer to an elder who was the primary leader over several churches in a given city. James may have occupied such a role in Jerusalem even before the end of the first century.

We must also remember that the organization of New Testament churches was influenced significantly by the organization of synagogues. Though a council of elders ruled over each synagogue, the Bible also speaks of those who were primary leaders in specific synagogues (Acts 18:8, 17).

From a practical standpoint it also seems wise to appoint one person as the primary leader in each church. This is particularly true as a church begins to grow and as staff pastors are added to the leadership team. Without designated lines of authority, insecurity frequently surfaces among the members of the church staff. Furthermore, the door is open for a power struggle to take place, which always results in disunity. Therefore, when an additional staff pastor is added, it is important that that individual be responsible to the senior spiritual leader. He cannot be equal in authority, for if he is, inefficiency and eventual conflict may result. In fact, on occasions nonstaff elders have created a power struggle with the staff pastor because they insist on trying to operate with equal authority. Nonstaff elders must be willing to give authority to the staff pastor as their primary leader. If they don't, again power struggles may develop. When a church is small and there is only one staff pastor, it is possible for him to function with a group of nonstaff elders as the church leaders. But even then, the staff pastor will and should emerge as an elder to the elders, a pastor to the pastors.

SERVANT LEADERSHIP

It is important to underscore the point that the more authority a spiritual leader has, the more he is to be a servant. He is not to lord it over those for whom he is responsible as leader. Though a leader, he is to serve the other pastoral staff members, the elders, and the entire congregation. Jesus demonstrated this principle when He taught that a person who is greatest is to be the servant of all (Matt. 23:11).

A staff pastor or a paid elder needs to have a submissive spirit toward the other nonstaff elders in the church. Though they look to him for leadership, he should also look to them for advice, counsel, and *overall* leadership. This is particularly true in an "elder-led" church. Though the elder board must delegate authority to the staff pastor to lead them, ultimately the board must have final authority over the senior pastor. Otherwise, he could become a law to himself, which is a dangerous position for any Christian leader and contradicts the principle of spiritual submissiveness so clearly taught in Scripture. As Jesus said to His disciples, "You know that the rulers of the Gentiles lord it over them and their high officials exercise authority over them. Not so with you. Instead, whoever wants to become great among you must be your servant, and whoever wants to be first must be your slave—just as the Son of Man did not come to be served, but to serve, and to give His life as a ransom for many" (Matt. 20:25–28).

8

Growth Strategies within the Local Church

OVER THE PAST FOUR DECADES many books on church growth have been published. Peter Wagner and Donald McGavran led the pack with some insightful volumes based on solid research. McGavran wrote *How Churches Grow* (1955), *Understanding Church Growth* (1970), and *How to Grow a Church* (1973; coauthored with Win Arn). And Wagner wrote *Your Church Can Grow* (1976), *Leading Your Church to Grow* (1984), and *The Healthy Church* (1996).

Our vision has been stretched and our direction more clearly focused by Robert Schuller's *Your Church Has Real Possibilities!* (1974), Frank Tillapaugh's *The Church Unleashed* (1982), Robert E. Logan's *Beyond Church Growth* (1989), George Barna's *User Friendly Churches* (1991), Jim Petersen's *Church without Walls* (1992), Leith Anderson's *A Church for the Twenty-First Century* (1992), and Rick Warren's *The Purpose Driven Church* (1995).

However, as a pastor I (Wall) have been most impacted by a European author, Christian A. Schwarz, whose research is succinctly presented in *Natural Church Development*.[1] Already this book has been published in nine languages. It is the result of research conducted in one thousand churches in thirty-two countries on five continents, including churches in the United States, South America, central and southern Africa, Europe, the former Soviet Union, India, Southeast Asia, and Australia. The study used research instruments developed over a ten-year period. A sampling of thirty church members was selected from each church. Growing and stagnant churches, charismatic and noncharismatic churches, and prominent and entirely unknown churches were included.

Although Schwarz overstates the connection between church growth and God's principles of growth in the natural world of plants and animals, his approach is a refreshing one that reflects most of the principles outlined in the preceding chapters and agrees with the scriptural priorities for the local church.

Following is a summary of Schwarz's eight principles of church growth, along with some pertinent biblical data and comments about their implications.

EIGHT QUALITIES OF A HEALTHY GROWING CHURCH

Schwarz argues that most church-growth theories tend toward either a "technocratic" or a "spiritualistic" approach. In the former "the significance of institutions, programs, methods, etc. is overestimated," and in the latter "the significance of institutions, programs, methods, etc. is underestimated."[2] His alternative is what he calls the "biotic paradigm," which reflects the realities of what the church is, as seen through theological lenses. Just as a plant will normally grow when it has rich soil, sufficient water, and sunshine, so a church, as an organism, will grow when the environment for growth is present.

Schwarz believes there are eight universal principles of church growth, that is, principles that are applicable in any culture. In introducing these principles, he made an insightful observation about the limited value of models and the need for universally valid principles.

A look at church growth literature can be confusing. An entire array of programs claim, "Do what we do, and you will get the same results." Unfortunately many of these concepts contradict one another. One group pushes "megachurches" as the most effective way to reach a community with the gospel, while another suggests that the optimal church size is a small group, almost like most home Bible studies. Some suggest that the key to success is a worship service targeted toward non-Christians, while others emphasize that the goal of a worship service is exclusively worshipping God and equipping the saints. One group is convinced that marketing strategies must be integrated into church planning, while another enjoys healthy church growth without even having heard of such methods.

It appears to me that past discussions have made too little distinction between "models" (=concepts, with which some church in some part of the world has had a positive experience) and "principles" (=that which applies to every church everywhere). Thus some models parade as universally valid principles. At the same time, proven principles with universal application are sometimes mistaken for "one model among many."[3]

Schwarz's research measured both the quality of the ministry of a given church and the level of quantitative growth or decline. By coordinating these two sets of data, he was able to correlate a given quality with four defined groups of churches: (a) "churches with above-average quality . . . and above-average quantitative growth in worship attendance," (b) "churches with above-average quality . . . but with diminishing worship attendance," (c) "churches with below-average quality . . . and diminishing worship attendance," and (d) "churches with below-average quality and above-average worship attendance."[4]

After ten years and five research projects Schwarz and his team in German-speaking Europe developed a research instrument that measured the qualities that they considered critical to the health of a church. From this worldwide research they were able to identify eight specific, universal church-growth principles. Further study revealed that any church that had a "quality index" (as reflected in the self-evaluation by a thirty-member sampling in each participating church) of sixty-five or over on a scale of one hundred in all eight growth qualities had a 99.4 percent potential for growth. *In other words, we need not focus our attention on growing numerically. Rather our attention should be centered on developing the qualities of a healthy church.* Even if Schwarz's biotic theory of church growth is not correct, his research does underscore the need for pastoral leaders to focus on strengthening the spiritual life of the church.

The trustworthiness of Schwarz's conclusions, nevertheless, requires a careful evaluation of each quality in the light of what the Bible promotes as healthy church life. His measurement of a particular quality, for example, may measure more the product of health than the cause of health.

Empowering Leadership

Instead of placing the responsibility and authority for the ministry exclusively on the pastor and his pastoral team, Schwarz observes that a healthy church empowers many in the congregation to take leadership. Many people believe that the leadership style of pastors in growing churches should be more project- than people-oriented, more goal- than relationship-oriented, more authoritarian- than team-oriented. However, Schwarz's findings indicate that most of these features have little effect on the growth of churches. He concludes that the key element in effective pastoral leadership is the empowering of other leaders in the church. Such pastors do not "use" people as "helpers," but rather equip, support, motivate, and mentor individuals, enabling them to become all God wants them to be. These pastors invest the majority of their time in discipleship, delegation, and multiplication.

Two other surprising observations were drawn from the data in this research. First, a pastor does not need to have a seminary education to help a church become healthy and growing. Of those pastors whose churches were healthy and growing only 42 percent had seminary degrees, and of those pastors whose churches were of a low quality and declining in attendance 85 percent had seminary degrees.[5]

Second, pastors of growing churches do not need to be superstars. Most of the pastors with the highest scores in the survey are not well known. "They generally provide us, however, with more helpful basic leadership principles than most of the world-famous 'spiritual superstars.'"[6]

Empowering leadership in the church is certainly biblical. Delegation is modeled in many contexts. Jethro exhorted his son-in-law, Moses, to delegate the responsibility of judging Israel to trustworthy men (Exod. 18:13–23). Both David and Solomon structured their kingdom with solid delegation (2 Sam. 20:23–26; 1 Kings 4:1–19). Nehemiah delegated many responsibilities in rebuilding the walls of Jerusalem (Neh. 3). In Jerusalem the early church faced the possibility of a major division over the distribution of church funds. The apostles solved the problem by appointing seven wise, spiritual men to administer the funds (Acts 6:1–6). As a result "the word of God spread, and the number of the disciples multiplied greatly in Jerusalem, and a great many of the priests were obedient to the faith" (6:7).

Gift-Oriented Ministry

Schwarz's second universal church-growth principle concerns spiritual gifts in the church. He explains, "The gift-oriented approach reflects the conviction that God sovereignly determines which Christians should best assume which ministries. The role of church leadership is to help its members to identify their gifts and to integrate them into appropriate ministries. . . . Unfortunately, in recent years some have misunderstood the gift-oriented approach as just another passing church growth fad. But the discovery and use of spiritual gifts is the only way to live out the Reformation watchword of the 'priesthood of all believers.'"[7] He then notes that it is stifling and often counterproductive for leaders to attempt "to dictate which ministries laypersons should assume and then search eagerly for 'volunteers.'"[8]

Whether a person accepts the existence of any or all of the spiritual gifts in the church today, everyone acknowledges that people in our churches need to function where they fit best and where they can be the most joyful and productive.

The Scriptures teach that each believer has at least one spiritual gift (1 Pet. 4:10–11). Every member of the body of Christ needs to be involved in the process of maturing others into Christlikeness, and certain gifts in the body equip them to do that (Eph. 4:11–16).

The challenge comes in developing effective ways to encourage people to understand what their gifts are and how they can most effectively be used in the body of Christ.

Passionate Spirituality

Schwarz explains this third principle this way: "Our research indicated clearly that church development is dependent neither on spiritual persuasions (such as charismatic or noncharismatic) nor on specific spiritual practices (such as liturgical prayers or 'spiritual warfare,' etc.) which are cited by some groups as the cause of church growth within their ranks. The point separating growing and nongrowing churches, those which are qualitatively above or below average, is a different one, namely: 'Are the Christians in this church "on fire"? Do they live committed lives and practice their faith with joy and enthusiasm?'"[9]

Orthodoxy alone, Schwarz adds, is not sufficient to produce growth. In fact, "wherever a 'defense of orthodoxy' replaces the expression of a passionate faith in Christ a false paradigm is at work. On such ideological ground, rigid fanaticism, but not truly liberated passion, will flourish."[10] Bill Bright puts it this way: "We want men and women in our movement who serve Christ with 'fire in their bellies.'"[11]

The Scriptures agree. God used Paul as a model of this kind of passion. To the Philippians he wrote, "For to me, to live is Christ and to die is gain.... But whatever was to my profit I now consider loss for the sake of Christ. What is more, I consider everything a loss compared to the surpassing greatness of knowing Christ Jesus my Lord, for whose sake I have lost all things. I consider them rubbish, that I may gain Christ and be found in him, not having a righteousness of my own that comes from the law, but that which is through faith in Christ—the righteousness that comes from God and is by faith. I want to know Christ and the power of his resurrection and the fellowship of sharing in his sufferings, becoming like him in his death, and so, somehow, to attain to the resurrection from the dead" (Phil. 1:21; 3:7–11).

Paul urged all believers to exercise this kind of passion for God and for their relationships with others in the church. "If you have any encouragement from being united with Christ, if any comfort from his love, if any fellowship with the Spirit, if any tenderness and compassion, then make my joy complete by being like-minded, having the same love, being one in spirit and purpose" (2:1–2).

Schwarz observes that spiritual passion is evidenced in two major ways: by church members being enthusiastic about their church, and by their having an "inspiring experience" in the prayer life of the church.

The challenge to church leaders is how to develop such a prayer life, especially in the context of changing attitudes and desires of the average believer. Here are a few of the changes in prayer over the past three decades, some of which are quite encouraging.

In the 1950s and 1960s	*In the 1990s*
Midweek prayer	Early morning prayer
Prayer warriors	Prayer intercessors
Cottage prayer	Small-group prayer
Little prayer education	Much prayer education
Pastoral prayer time	Individual prayer time
A strength of churches	A weakness in churches
Pastors lead in prayer	Directors of prayer lead
Prayer at the end of counseling	Prayer as an ingredient of counseling
Obligation to pray	Burden to pray
Prayer lists	Prayer journaling
Praying defensively	Praying offensively
Opening prayers for a service	Prayer teams during the service
Prayer partners	Prayer triads
Low profile for prayer	High prayer visibility[12]

Churches have responded with some fresh approaches to prayer: praying the Scriptures, concerts of prayer, praise services, on-site praying (for example, students meeting to pray at their school's flagpole), emphasis on spiritual warfare, prayer partners and triads, small-group prayer, prayer seminars, prayer retreats, early morning prayer, prayer walks, identification of intercessors, and team prayer (for example, the pastoral staff).[13]

In their church-growth newsletter Glenn Martin and Gary McIntosh offer ten suggestions for improving a church's prayer life:

1. Pray about everything—decisions, problems, giving thanks, prayer for each other, asking His blessing and guidance before each ministry activity.
2. Encourage significant staff and leaders to pray—possibly "require staff to set aside time each day for personal prayer. Once each week, bring the staff together to pray for each other, your church and the needs of the congregation."

3. Organize prayer partners.
4. Integrate prayer into your small groups.
5. Include prayer as an agenda item in all church meetings.
6. Conduct prayer seminars.
7. Hold leadership prayer retreats.
8. Offer early morning prayer times.
9. Develop prayer opportunities in Sunday school.
10. Encourage leaders to read resources on prayer.[14]

Functional Structures

When Schwarz describes "functional structures," he makes three major points. First, structures need to reflect function, and they need to be readily changed to meet functional needs. Second, structures should enhance the selection and training of leaders, and thus promote ongoing multiplication of the ministry. Third, traditionalism, a major hindrance to growth, needs to be diminished in its control of a church. Schwarz discovered that half of the churches that had low-quality ministry and declining attendance indicated that traditionalism was a major characteristic of their church. However, of the high-quality, growing churches only 8 percent said they had problems with traditionalism.[15]

The Scriptures also reveal the dangers of traditionalism. Jesus often attacked the traditionalism of the Pharisees and Sadducees, and it was this same legalistic traditionalism that drove the Jewish leaders to have Him crucified.

To remember and recognize one's heritage requires respect for some traditions. However, when tradition becomes a controlling element in the life of a church, it can be a dangerous inhibitor to following the Lord and being able to respond adequately to the functional needs of the church. Traditionalism has kept some churches from modifying their children's and youth programs to include creative approaches to evangelism. Traditionalism has kept women's ministries from changing and expanding to meet the needs of working women.[16] Traditionalism about church meeting times has hamstrung many older churches from developing effective small-group ministries.

Inspiring Worship Services

The term *inspiring* is used in the sense of "in-breathing," that is, having services in which people experience the in-breathing of the Holy Spirit. The style or form of worship service is not the key to making a church grow. Whether the services are so-called "seeker services," or are liturgical, or in-between, the key issue for true growth is whether the Holy Spirit is at work in the services.[17]

The New Testament says little about worship forms and style of music in church services. But Paul emphasized in Ephesians 5:18–19 that music in the church is to be the product of the Spirit's filling.

It is good to be reminded of this principle. However, church leaders today face major issues as they seek to provide worship services that encourage and enhance the individual's response to the Spirit of God. Cultural diversity is growing within our churches, especially between the generations, and it is becoming increasingly difficult for leaders to minister adequately to the entire body of believers.

Churches are attempting different options with varying success: (a) different worship styles in separate morning services; (b) an alternate service on Sunday evenings or another day of the week; (c) a blended service that attempts to meet the needs of a large spectrum of the church; (d) special evangelistic services, such as concerts, geared for particular target groups; and (e) a church plant with a different style of worship aimed at a different cultural group.

In its School of Evangelism the Billy Graham Evangelistic Organization suggests that churches attempt to have "blended" worship styles in their services, that is, a combination of traditional hymns, contemporary music, and classical music, trying to avoid extremes of any kind that would hinder the worship of major segments of the congregation. Then the church should schedule other times in which the entire music is targeted for specific groups—perhaps a Sunday evening hymn sing or a Friday night "praise and worship" concert.

Church leaders facing the challenge of planning worship services for a changing and diverse congregation might want to consider the following suggestions. First, the pastor needs to teach (a) the difference between form and function, (b) what it means to live under grace, (c) how to love those who have differing tastes and convictions, and (d) ways to look out for the interests of others more than their own (Rom. 14:1–15:3; Phil. 2:1–5). Second, prayer teams need to focus their prayers on the services and the attitudes of the attendees. Third, if changes are needed that will enhance the church's ability to reach larger numbers of people, changes need to be done in small increments with much celebration of the benefits of the changes. Fourth, appoint a worship service planning team, made up of people representing various age groups, to design the weekly worship services.

Holistic Small Groups

Schwarz's study shows that "continuous multiplication of small groups is a universal church-growth principle. . . . Such groups, however, must be *holistic* groups which go beyond just discussing Bible passages to applying its message to daily life. In these groups, members are able to bring up those issues and questions that are immediate personal concerns."[18]

This factor is certainly a biblical one. Small groups were important in the growth of the early church (Acts 2:46–47). The Epistles indicate that small groups are key to the church's ability to carry out the scriptural directives for healthy church relationships and spiritual growth. Two major passages in the New Testament describe the spiritual-growth process. Hebrews 5:12–14 emphasizes that spiritual growth takes place when people are fed the truth and then obey it. Ephesians 4:11–16 explains that growth happens when leaders utilize their spiritual gifts and believers have opportunity to interact with the truth in a loving context. We might illustrate the elements in the biblical pattern by a picket fence with the pickets attached to two rows of boards. The top row of boards represents the communication of truth (cognitive input). The bottom of row of boards represents the application of the truth (behavioral output). The pickets that connect the two rows of boards represent interaction about the truth and its application. Small groups provide loving contexts for this kind of interaction. They also provide the environment in which healthy church relationships are cultivated—the place where the "one anothers" of Scripture can readily be experienced.

Need-Oriented Evangelism

Contradicting conventional wisdom about evangelism, Schwarz's research drew some interesting conclusions. First, in growing churches the leaders know which congregants have the gift of evangelism, and they direct them into appropriate ministry areas. (Some church leaders have suggested that about 10 percent of the believers in an average congregation have the gift of evangelism.) Second, the congregation at large is not pressured to imitate those with the gift of evangelism. Third, church members are taught to have a part in carrying out the Great Commission, using their strengths and relationships. They are encouraged to focus on the questions and needs of non-Christians and to use their sovereignly bestowed gift (or gifts) to serve non-Christians they know.[19] This process implies that all church members should be trained to communicate the gospel clearly.

Need-oriented evangelism might look something like this: Church members are present at the hospital when a neighbor's child is sick. Church members provide a safe and fun place for the neighborhood kids to play. They spend time playing (tennis, golf, bunko, etc.) with their neighbors and are active in groups like Big Brothers or the Scouts. They tutor in public schools and minister to the homeless, to the hospitalized, to the unemployed, to those addicted to alcohol or drugs, and to immigrants who cannot speak English well. The church provides childcare for single mothers, training in child rearing, and exercise and weight-loss classes. It also provides a ministry to those whose marriages are struggling and to single parents. What an impact these ministries can have, when accompanied by a clear communication of the gospel!

The principle of need-oriented evangelism is clearly taught in Scripture. True spiritual growth in the church issues from the functioning of the different spiritual gifts in the body (Eph. 4:11–16). And the early church grew as believers experienced favor in the eyes of the watching world (Acts 5:13–14). However, the New Testament also describes aggressive evangelistic methods and strategies. Paul's strategy included targeting particular groups and taking advantage of every opportunity to proclaim the gospel. He normally went first to the synagogues to speak (13:14; 14:1). He witnessed in jail through song (16:25). He accepted an invitation to speak to the philosophers of the Areopagus in Athens (17:19–31). And he declared the gospel in the presence of a mob and before judges and rulers (21:30–22:21; 23:1–6; 24:10–21; 26:1–29).

This principle of Schwarz's reminds us of some important elements in mobilizing a local church in evangelism. A biblical strategy must include the use of aggressive evangelistic methods.

Loving Relationships

On average, Schwarz writes, growing churches have a high "love quotient." This includes members spending time with each other apart from official church-sponsored events—inviting others over for a cup of coffee. It also includes the pastoral staff being aware of and showing concern for individuals' problems. And it includes enjoying each other's company and even laughing together.[20]

Loving relationships in the church are of paramount importance in the Scriptures. Jesus taught that the two greatest commandments involve love (Matt. 22:37–39). Virtually every New Testament epistle exhorts believers to love each other and to care for each other. It is not surprising that loving relationships are vital for church growth. After all, love as discussed in chapter 3, draws people together, much as a magnet attracts iron.

Schwarz, then, suggests that these eight factors are essential for meaningful church growth.

Eight Elements Needed for Meaningful Church Growth

- Empowering leadership
- Gift-oriented ministry
- Passionate spirituality
- Functional structures
- Inspiring worship services
- Holistic small groups
- Need-oriented evangelism
- Loving relationships

Implications

Schwarz concludes with three major implications of these principles. First, "the qualitative approach, as described in the previous sections, has tremendous significance for practical ministry. Our fundamental question is not, 'How do we attract more people to our worship service?' but rather, 'How can we grow in each of the eight quality areas?' Behind this question is the solid conviction—both theologically and empirically founded—that genuine quality will ultimately positively impact quantitative growth."[21]

Second, against the common notion that "developing quantity requires a *different* set of methods than developing quality," we can be confident that "precisely the same 'methods' which produce higher quality will generate quantitative growth as a natural 'by-product.' "[22]

Third, small churches proportionately develop and mobilize individual spiritual gifts far better than larger churches, and small churches proportionately lead far more people to Christ than do larger churches.[23] Of course, effective small churches will become larger churches, but these facts should motivate us to emphasize the multiplication of churches through church planting.

FOUR ADDITIONAL QUALITIES OF A BIBLICALLY HEALTHY CHURCH

Schwarz has pinpointed eight important qualities that generally correlate with biblical examples and teaching of what a spiritually healthy church looks like. In addition, the Scriptures reveal at least four other characteristics of a healthy church.

Biblical Preaching and Teaching

The example of the apostolic preaching in the Book of Acts and the clear injunctions of the New Testament writers make it clear that the spiritual health of God's people, and thus of His churches, requires an understanding of and application of the truths of God's Word. Paul taught the influential Ephesian church the whole counsel of God (Acts 20:27), and he exhorted young Timothy to "preach the Word" in whatever situation he was called to minister (2 Tim. 4:2). Only God's Word can feed the soul (Matt. 4:4), and only God's truth communicated in the context of love can produce spiritual growth (Eph. 4:14–16).

Visionary and Spiritual Leaders

Developing spiritually healthy churches requires the leadership of vision- ary and spiritual pastors, elders, and deacons. The church leaders need to be spiritual men and women of wisdom and integrity, who have an inti- mate, authentic walk with God (Acts 6:1–3; 1 Tim. 3:1–13; Titus 1:6–9). They need to be men who seek direction from God and who are willing to take steps of faith through doors of opportunity (1 Cor. 16:8–9; Rev. 3:8). The most effective evangelistic missionary endeavor in the first cen- tury sprang from a prayer meeting of church leaders (Acts 13:1–3). Church leaders also need to be deeply concerned for the welfare of the flock, serv- ing unselfishly, leading by example, and not lording over the congregation (1 Pet. 5:2–3). Such leaders are sensitive to God's direction, and the con- gregation is willing to trust their leadership. As Robert Logan, of Church Resource Ministries, wrote, "It is the personal vision of a pastor or church planter, and his or her ability to communicate that vision, that drives churches to growth."[24]

Unity

Division in a local church hobbles its ministry and prevents or restricts growth. Paul made it clear that church unity is related to growth (Eph. 4:3–6; 12–13).

Achieving unity in the church is seldom easy. In my first pastorate after seminary I was faced with significant conflict in the church. Several major theological issues concerning grace and legalism and the nature of the body of Christ had divided the church. For months several members and I prayed for unity. Then God answered in a remarkable way. Several families left the church for various reasons, and the remaining families were knit together in warm fellowship. The church was then freed up to move forward with aggressive evangelistic ministries. Today that little church has grown to become a large, grace-oriented church with regional and worldwide influence.

Although doctrinal issues can divide churches, more often divisiveness stems from selfish attitudes, hurt feelings, and worship-service preferences. Because church unity is important, it is necessary to take time and energy to address these issues and work toward reconciling estranged Christian brothers and sisters.

When issues that are potentially divisive arise, they need to be addressed quickly, graciously, and firmly. In such situations leaders need to model and teach the principles of Philippians 2:3–4: "Do nothing out of selfish ambition or vain conceit, but in humility consider others better than yourselves. Each of you should look not only to your own interests, but also to the interests of others."

Stewardship

For a church to meet the challenges necessary for growth, funds are needed, and funding a church requires that the members of the congregation be good stewards.

In many churches, teaching on stewardship comes across as pressuring or shaming people into giving. In other churches, pastors seldom if ever mention money or stewardship, for fear of offending church members or visitors.

Neither of these approaches is acceptable biblically. On the one hand, Paul taught that giving should not be pressured (2 Cor. 8:2–3; 9:5, 7). On the other hand, both he and Jesus instructed believers to give sacrificially (Matt. 6:19–21, 24; 2 Cor. 8:7; 9:5–6, 13).

Timothy Hawks, pastor of the Hill Country Bible Church of Austin, Texas, maintains that there are three major ingredients in the development of healthy stewardship in a congregation.[25] First, the leaders of the church need to model good stewardship. Second, the church needs to spend time as families and as a congregation praying about the needs of the church and their own part in meeting those needs. Third, the church needs to be taught what the Bible says about stewardship. Following are five important stewardship principles:

- All that we have belongs to God (Ps. 24:1); we are only stewards of what we possess (1 Cor. 4:2).
- We are to be content with what God provides for us (1 Tim. 6:6–7).
- We are to manage well all that He has given us (Col. 3:23–24).
- We are to give regularly and systematically to ministries He holds dear (Prov. 3:9; 1 Cor. 16:1–2).
- We are to excel in our giving (2 Cor. 8:7).[26]

Without solid teaching on stewardship, growth in local churches may be limited.

NINE FACTORS TO ADDRESS WHEN APPLYING CHURCH-GROWTH PRINCIPLES

Any experienced pastor knows that understanding the principles that universally produce church growth is not enough. Several practical issues must be faced. Following are some of the factors that need to be addressed when attempting to implement growth principles.

Demographics

Understanding the demographics of your community and how it compares with your church's constituency is important as you plan for growth. Students of church growth have noted that growth usually accompanies homogenous relationships. Although churches are meant to be expressions of the heterogeneous body of Christ, evangelism most readily takes place between people who have things in common, and people are attracted to churches in which they feel most comfortable. We can decry this reality, but we must face this fact in our efforts to reach a community for Christ.[27]

The analysis of your congregation should include age, marital status, race, and socioeconomic characteristics. The demographic research of your community should include these same factors, noting the current and projected population. It should also include data on other churches in the area, schools, plans for business expansion, and special needs in the community such as day care, help with drug addiction, English language classes, and the like. This data should not be used to reinforce unbiblical division in the church but should provide guidance in developing need-oriented evangelism and services geared to meet the needs of the community.

Sometimes the community in which a church serves changes racially or culturally. It may become advisable to develop special services for various racial groups. A church in Houston was started as a rural church, ministering largely to English-speaking German Americans. As the city and the church grew, the church became a suburban church ministering to middle class and upper-middle-class Anglos. Then Hispanic and Asian families began to dominate the immediate community. So the church began Hispanic, Korean, and Vietnamese churches within the facility.

Advertising

Some churches find advertising to be a useful tool for enhancing church growth. Newspaper ads, a regular radio or television program, and yellow pages help new people in your community who are looking for a particular kind of church to find yours. Mailings to newcomers often help bring in visitors. Billboards can draw people to a particular ministry you provide, and they give you exposure to new people in your community as well. Signs, posters, and local newspaper ads can be used to invite targeted groups to special ministries such as those provided for the deaf, non-English-speaking immigrants, and single parents.

Evangelistic Methods and Tools

Opportunities abound for evangelism. For children, evangelism tools include Sunday school, backyard Bible clubs, vacation Bible school, Child Evangelism clubs, and camps. For youth, evangelistic opportunities are available in Sunday school, fun nights, Bible studies, trips, camping, and campus contacts. Means for reaching adults for Christ include concerts, "Jesus" video distribution, follow-up of Sunday visitors, mailings, door-to-door visitation, home Bible studies, church Bible classes, welcome service to new residences, evangelistic coffees and dinners, and meetings for special needs such as weight loss and marriage building.

How can a church decide which means to use, and how can a church mobilize members of the congregation to become involved? Here are a few suggestions:

1. Don't try to do everything at once.
2. Stress need-oriented evangelism.
3. Build a team of people with administrative gifts who can manage the projects well.
4. Encourage those who have the gift of evangelism to be linked with believers who have administrative gifts to carry out various projects.
5. Delegate responsibilities.
6. Keep the church informed of evangelism results.
7. Develop special-occasion activities, such as a special Easter program or an evangelistic meeting with an illusionist.
8. Provide training in how believers can share their faith and communicate their testimonies.

Assimilation

A church may have effective evangelism in the community and great ministries to the church body, but growth can be limited if new people are not assimilated into the church's life.

Assimilation begins when a visitor drives into your church's parking lot. Attractive, easy-to-understand signs (including posted maps of your facilities) will minimize the feeling of disorientation. Well-marked parking places for visitors, the handicapped, seniors, and single parents can also make visitors feel welcome.

Greeters on the parking lots and in the foyer of the auditorium (possibly at an information booth) are a great help, and greeters in the Sunday-school classes are also important. Some churches recognize visitors in their worship services. This can be especially helpful, if it is done in a way that does not embarrass the guests. Brochures or packets of information for guests are common tools in visitor-sensitive churches, and it is always helpful to get new people to fill out visitors cards so you can follow up with letters from the pastor and appropriate ministry leaders, and/or with a personal visit. Some churches assign hosts for different parts of the auditorium, whose assignment is to try to spot newcomers and visit with them before and after the services.

New attenders might be invited to a brief social time with the pastor after the Sunday-morning service or to have lunch with the pastor and his wife or some other leader and his or her spouse. Or several individuals in a Bible class may invite visitors to join them as their guests at a restaurant for Sunday lunch. Mailing a card to visitors and/or telephoning or visiting them during the week are ways to let newcomers know they are welcome.

Also young people should be encouraged to be especially friendly to teens visiting their Sunday-school class. Many youth in our churches need this reminder because it is easy for them to be cliquish and to snub or ignore "outsiders."

New attenders can also be encouraged to attend a one-session class near the auditorium, in which they can be introduced to the church, its message, and its ministries. Attenders at this class can then be directed to a class for new people in which the gospel and basic doctrines are made clear, the basics of the spiritual life are taught, and the people are oriented to the best way they can be trained for Christian service. This is a great way for newcomers to get to know the pastoral staff and get acquainted with other people. It can also help them begin to discover their spiritual gifts and how they can use them in ministry.

Then the new people can be encouraged to join a regular Sunday-school class and/or become involved in a particular Sunday ministry. It is also helpful to assign a couple to shepherd one or two new couples during the first year of involvement in the church, to help the new ones get to know others in the church and to become involved in a small group and in a place of service. As people become involved in these activities and relationships, they are more likely to become a part of the local church and less likely to leave and go elsewhere. This is a significant but often-neglected aspect of church growth.

Some larger churches are finding it helpful to hire a part-time or full-time minister of assimilation responsible for coordinating these activities, for noting and welcoming visitors, and for seeking to make them a part of the church.

Momentum

Momentum is an amazing phenomenon. It is difficult to reverse a church that is in decline. Conversely it is difficult to stop the growth of a church that is growing and in which the people are excited about what God is doing.

A number of years ago Lew Worrad, missionary to the former Soviet Union, took the pastorate of an old church in Hamilton, Ontario. The church had a building that would seat one thousand, but the attendance was two hundred seventy. He was convinced that they needed to reverse their thinking and to enhance their momentum. Two years in a row they invited special groups to put on a Christmas program, and the church was filled to capacity at those services. From that point on the church began to climb in attendance.

How depressing it can be for people to talk continually about what they don't like in their church or how it was better in the past or in another church. While in seminary I pastored a small church near Dallas. The church had a weekly attendance of about thirty. When I suggested that we have a vacation Bible school, I was told there were not enough children in the community, and no one would teach in the Bible school anyway. To get the momentum going I invited a group of teenagers from a suburban church in Richardson, Texas, to assist me. We held vacation Bible school at 5:00 P.M., followed by evening evangelistic meetings led by a fellow student at Dallas Seminary. During the day he and I went door to door in the town and in the countryside, visiting with people. Every afternoon over fifty people came to the Bible school, and the church was packed each night. On the following Sunday we baptized about thirty new believers. Now we had some momentum!

In 1984 I was asked to take the presidency of Western Bible College near Denver. Enrollment had dropped to one hundred thirty-five, and the board of directors was considering closing the school. At the end of my first year we graduated about a dozen students. In that extremely difficult year a small Christian liberal arts school, Rockmont College, merged with Western Bible College, and next fall we opened with a student body of approximately three hundred. I was told that it was impossible for a Christian college in Colorado to grow beyond four hundred students because the state's Christian student population was small.

I sensed that the school needed some momentum. When registration came in at less than four hundred the next year, I started a nighttime class that I personally taught and that I advertised on the school's radio station. That class helped our total enrollment surpass four hundred, and I knew we had the beginning of momentum. People began to believe that a larger school was possible. Then we merged with a small Southern Baptist extension school and acquired a graduate program in biblical counseling. Within eight years we had expanded to four campuses in the state with over two thousand students. Today the annual enrollment is approximately three thousand on five campuses. Momentum is critical to growth.

Special-Interest Groups

Any experienced pastor immediately recognizes that special-interest groups contribute to growth. By this I mean ministries that are directed to specific groups in the church and in the community.

Ministering to certain groups—such as to children and youth—is critical for the survival of most churches. The more effective these ministries are, the stronger the attraction of families to the church.

The addition of new specific ministries can appreciably expand the impact of the church and generate a significant jump in attendance. New ministries to consider are those that focus on singles (both college and career singles and older singles), young married couples, the formerly married, divorce recovery groups, grief recovery groups, the elderly, families with physically impaired members, and people needing translation into their national languages.

Location

Realtors often point out that there are three major considerations in buying real estate: location, location, and location. This is not necessarily the case with church growth, but location is definitely important. Three important factors to be considered in choosing a location for a church building are exposure, access, and expansion.

Exposure. Try to find a piece of property that allows for exposure to the public. But even if the property is not on a main avenue, sometimes property can be situated so that it is close enough to a main thoroughfare that a nearby sign can give sufficient exposure.

Access. A church needs to be easily accessible by the people in the target-area population. Purchasing property on a major freeway might provide good exposure, but be careful that it doesn't significantly restrict good access.

Expansion. Where possible, buy property that will allow for expansion at a future date. Although churches can move, it can be a traumatic experience for a congregation.

Facilities

Churches can grow without buildings. However, certain cultural characteristics and political and economic realities usually make ownership of facilities necessary. In most cases in the United States church buildings are a sign of stability and in some cases a sign of ministry quality. In other countries, such as the former Soviet Union, governmental pressure makes it very difficult to rent facilities, so it becomes necessary to own a building.

Renting facilities is usually necessary when a church begins, but renting is not without its problems. Often churches must bring in chairs and baby beds each week, as storage facilities are usually limited. The janitor of the school in Houston where we were meeting had the only key to the facilities, and occasionally he overslept, leaving us out in the cold. If the church does not have a long-term lease, the rented facilities can be sold or leased out from under the church. I started a church in Garland, Texas, in the 1970s in an office-warehouse complex that had been empty for years. But within a few months after we moved in we were forced to move again. We moved three times in two years, and the rent far exceeded what it would have cost us to buy. With all the moves we found ourselves greatly limited in growth as well. Not until the church purchased a permanent church building was it able to stabilize and grow.

When you build, consider the factors listed below.

Factors to Consider When Planning to Build

- Build after having developed a long-range plan for both ministries and facilities.
- Build facilities that can have multiple use as much as possible.
- Build functional buildings, but keep the quality at a level that provides a good testimony and saves future expenses in upkeep.
- Set wise practical limits on borrowing money.
- Do not build with the idea that a building will make the church grow; rather build to meet the needs of a growing church.
- Build so that buildings can be expanded at a later date.

Priorities

In planning ways to address the spiritual health of a church, pastors and church leaders are often overwhelmed. It is usually helpful to prioritize one's objectives and then attack a few needs at a time.

Early in my ministry an older pastor advised me to focus on two ministries of the church: one that is already going well and can be celebrated and strengthened, and one that is not going well but is needed for the health of the church and its witness.

Timothy Hawks shared with me that each year he has led his church (Hill Country Bible Church, Austin, Texas) to adopt one major focus for the year. One year it was the development of small groups, and the leadership made a strong push to get virtually everyone in the church into small groups. Another year it was stewardship, and they raised funds sufficient for the construction of a new facility. This is a good practice. Select one or two of the areas that need to be addressed and prayerfully begin the process of bringing the leaders together to agree on a focus for each year.

SUMMARY

The qualities of a healthy church and the factors for implementing these qualities outlined in this chapter can form a helpful framework for planning and evaluating a church's ministries.

There are, however, a number of other factors over which the church leader may have little or no control that can affect church growth. A church that is in a growing community is more likely to grow than one in a community that is changing in its racial and socioeconomic makeup. Churches riding the crest of a regional revival will usually experience growth.

Also it should be remembered that each church is distinct and in some ways unique. Therefore the principles one draws from this study can never take the place of humbly seeking the Lord's face and responding obediently with courageous faith to His leading for *one's own* church. Wise pastors avoid comparing their churches with other churches, and they avoid mimicking other churches. Aware of the biblical qualities of a healthy church, wise pastors lead their people in the way they believe the Chief Shepherd is leading them and their flocks.

9

Church Growth by Multiplication

*C*HURCH GROWTH (both spiritual and numerical) can take place within established local churches. But churches can also grow by multiplication: through church planting, pastoral training in the church, and effective missionary efforts.

THE PRINCIPLE OF MULTIPLICATION

Vision-minded people are always looking for ways to multiply their efforts. Businessmen, for example, try to grow their businesses by enlarging their markets. My son works for a company that sets up seasonally oriented stores in shopping malls. When the company started, it opened one store and then added a few more stores; they grew slowly. This is growth by addition. Then they added new cities by franchising local owners, and their business and profits began to balloon exponentially. This is multiplication. Multilevel marketing strategies also employ the multiplication principle.

Vision-minded evangelists think "multiplication." This is why Bill Bright of Campus Crusade for Christ is always trying to make his teaching materials "transferable."

If we lead someone to Christ and then train him to lead someone else while we continue to evangelize others, and if the same process is followed generation after spiritual generation, then the multiplication principle is implemented. If this same process were repeated annually for thirty-two years, there would be more than four billion new believers in the world, roughly the equivalent of the unbelieving population of the world today.

The principle of multiplication is best illustrated by an offer I make to students in evangelism and church-planting classes. If you were asked to choose between receiving one thousand dollars a day for thirty days or receiving one dollar and having the dollar doubled every day for a month, which would you choose? Receiving one thousand dollars for each of thirty days results in thirty thousand dollars. But multiplying one dollar for thirty days would produce more than a billion dollars—$1,073,741,824, to be exact![1]

MULTIPLICATION THROUGH CHURCH PLANTING

In 2 Timothy 2:2, Paul presented the concept of multiplication: "And the things you have heard me say in the presence of many witnesses entrust to reliable men who will also be qualified to teach others." This passage is usually applied to person-to-person evangelism and follow-up. However, the primary thrust in the context relates to the multiplication of local-church leadership and, by implication, the multiplication of churches.

The principle of multiplication involves producing new churches that will be able to produce more new churches while the original church is beginning still another church.

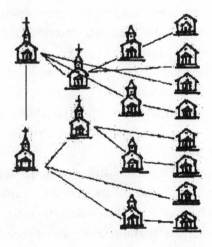

Church multiplication is the process of church planting by geometric proportions—churches planting churches, which in turn plant new churches while the mother church continues to plant churches.

A reasonable application of this strategy in the United States would be to plan for the planting of a new church, on the average, every three years. Each new church would be expected in turn to reproduce itself by the end of the next three years. In thirty years over one thousand churches would be planted, as the following pattern shows:

First three years	2 churches
Second three years	4 churches
Third three years	8 churches
Fourth three years	16 churches
Fifth three years	32 churches
Sixth three years	64 churches
Seventh three years	128 churches
Eighth three years	256 churches
Ninth three years	512 churches
Tenth three years	1024 churches

Of course, for many reasons this pattern breaks down. But some churches are effectively applying this exciting strategy on a limited scale.

In one city two solid, evangelical, older churches called new pastors at about the same time. One of the churches, pastored by an exceptional evangelistic preacher, was the "First" church of the denomination in the city. It had been on a decline and was down to five hundred in Sunday worship attendance. The other church, pastored by a fairly average preacher, had about two hundred seventy in the Sunday morning services. Within a decade the first church had grown to a Sunday attendance of over four thousand. The smaller church began to plant churches and to encourage each of them to plant more churches, resulting in multiplication. So within a decade the total attendance in the mother church and the more than twenty planted churches[2] had grown to approximately eight thousand in Sunday services. God blessed both methods, and both churches continue to have a positive impact on the city. This illustrates that those who are not so greatly gifted as others can still have a significant impact on church growth, if they have a vision for multiplication.

Kinds of Church Planting

Church planting in the early church was carried out in at least three ways: branch church planting, colonization church planting, and pioneer (or missionary) church planting.

Branch church planting: Spinning off members from a mother church. As the church at Jerusalem grew, believers met in house-church units. Today a local assembly could consider taking a group of families (including some leaders) from an existing church and starting a new church in a nearby community. Some pastors say a church should begin taking steps toward founding a branch work when the mother church has about 250 or 300 regular attendees. But does this reduce the size of the founding church? Perhaps at first. But usually a maturing church continues to grow even when it starts another church. Evidence of this is seen in the fact that a good number of churches that have started branch works maintain membership numbering in the hundreds and even thousands of people.

Another plan is for a growing church to establish satellite churches (a plan being used effectively by some Baptist churches). A satellite church meets in a different location from the original church, but it shares the same leaders and pastoral staff. The preaching staff is rotated regularly among the cluster of churches.

Colonization church planting: Intentionally or unintentionally relocating a core group from another church to plant in a new community. By sovereign design, many in the original Jerusalem church were forced to move to new locations. The church at Antioch (Acts 11:19–21) sprang from those "transplanted" believers.

A local church might consider placing a group of families in a new location where a church is needed. For example, some families might move into an apartment complex that is closed to a gospel witness. An easier approach is to map out the residences of the present membership and begin a work in a community where some members live a greater distance from the mother church.

Pioneer (or missionary) church planting: Starting a new church from scratch. The Holy Spirit moved on the church at Antioch, and the first planned Christian missionary tour among the Gentiles was born (13:1–3).

Church planting can be done by a missionary in two ways. He can gather a group of Christians already living in a new location, contacting them through visits, publicity, and specialized ministries. Or he can do pioneer evangelistic work and then gather the new believers into an assembly.

Other kinds of church planting. Robert Logan and Steven Ogne suggest some other forms of church planting. These are three of them:

> *Adopting:* A larger church is approached by a group who wants to begin a church and needs assistance.
>
> *Partnering.* Several churches and/or denominational or mission agencies cooperate in starting a new church.
>
> *Revitalizing.* A larger church assists a struggling older church to get on its feet again.

Steps in Planting a Church

In the one hundred or more church-planting situations in which I have been directly involved or have trained church planters, I have found that planting a church is like planting a bush or flower. You must prepare the soil *(the preparation stage)*, plant the seed *(the seed-planting stage)*, feed and water the seed *(the sapling stage)*, and continue to feed and water the plant *(the full-grown plant stage)*.

The preparation stage. Before beginning a new church some important steps need to be taken by the sponsoring church and/or the core group.

- If a sponsoring church is involved, the congregation needs to be committed to the project.
- Determine the area in which the church will be established.
- Determine the doctrine and structure of the new work and set up plans to safeguard the doctrine. (See the list of potential problems that begins on page 130 and the sample constitution in Appendix E).
- Discuss the philosophy of ministry, the priorities of the new work, and the kinds of services to be held.

Following are some of the issues that need to be addressed early in the process:

Is there a need for a new church? To the idea of starting another church, some may say, "Why do we need another church? Don't we have enough churches already? What we really need is revival in our existing churches."

Many reasons support the need to start new churches. First, existing churches have not saturated the population of most communities with their message and ministry. Second, population growth continues to demand the establishment of new Christian assemblies. Third, some unreached cultural groups in many communities have special needs. Fourth, in many communities some evangelical churches are bound by an introverted mentality that hinder their making a significant impact on the world. Fifth, liberal theology has virtually eradicated the communication of a clear gospel in many churches. Sixth, many areas, though blessed with "gospel-preaching" churches, are deprived of significant Bible teaching.

Church planters, however, need to evaluate carefully the need in a given area. A new church should never intentionally drain members from another evangelical witness in the area. Obviously some of the "core leadership" will come from other evangelical churches, but the growth needs to be projected on the basis of need.

What are your church-growth goals? Early in the process of developing a church-planting ministry, the responsible persons involved need to develop long-range and short-range goals. These should relate to the needs of the surrounding communities and should include a time schedule for establishing new churches. Any long-range planning should seriously consider both geographical and cultural factors in a community. An honest attempt should be made to recognize the effectiveness of other evangelical ministries in the area, to avoid needless competition and duplication.

What are you trying to multiply? Care needs to be taken to plant the best possible kind of church from the beginning. During early goal-setting sessions, it would be helpful to list the characteristics desired in the new work. Following is a list of subjects that should be considered.

- *Doctrine.* A clear doctrinal statement (either a summary statement of faith, or complete articles prepared in advance for the church consistution) should be devised.
- *Relationship to other churches and church bodies.* Is the new work to

become a part of a denomination or fellowship of churches, or is it to be an autonomous organization? What will be the new church's relationship to its mother church?

- *Local church government.* Will the new church be governed by a board, congregational meetings, a pastor, or a combination of these? Will the church have a voting membership, nonvoting membership, or no official membership?
- *Kind of ministry.* Wise church planters seek to establish churches that balance the following elements: vital learning experiences with the Word of God (teaching and exhortation); vital relational experiences with each other (fellowship by sharing needs, blessings, and ministries); vital outreach experiences in a fallen world (evangelism, missions, and influence on society); and vital worship and fellowship experiences with God (praise and prayer).
- *Ministry structure.* Will the leaders (elders) carry on an active ministry to meet the needs of people. Will the church emphasize family time or church meetings? Will it allow for and encourage the free exercise of the edifying spiritual gifts? How will evangelism be carried on? Will it be through the Sunday morning services primarily, through a planned church outreach, or through the spontaneous outreach of the people? What forms will the new church implement to develop significant caring among the members—mini-churches, flock groups, fellowship groups, prayer groups, home Bible studies, sharing times in the services?

What will it cost? A question often asked in the planning stage of church-planting efforts is "What will it cost in time, money, and personnel?" These factors vary, depending on the approach taken.

A sponsoring church will need to release both leaders and workers from other major responsibilities for the first three to six months to give time to the new work.

Financial needs will vary from church to church. In some cases a young church will get off the ground quickly and need no more than a month's rent for temporary quarters. In other cases a pioneer ministry will need full support for several months, and partial support up to two years. However, financial limitations should not prevent a church from developing a new work. By using homes or other free meeting places, some new church plants may need little or no financial help. Financial assistance by itself does not guarantee growth. In fact some church planters have observed that some of the strongest church plants started with very limited financial resources.

The most significant contribution you can make to a new church is people—especially potential leaders. This is also the greatest sacrifice a sponsoring church can make—providing leaders from their own numbers. Here is where the immediate impact on the sponsoring church needs to be evaluated carefully. However, we should remember that Christ, as Lord of the church, will remain faithful to His people, especially those who give sacrificially for the work of the ministry.

The seed-planting stage. This stage includes two steps: evangelizing the lost and gathering interested believers, and pre-Sunday-service meetings.

In many cases a new work will involve some preliminary contact with the community to locate interested Christians. In other cases the primary emphasis will be on pioneer evangelism. Following are a few suggestions for carrying out this first stage.

- Use newspapers, radio, and TV to announce the new church or the preliminary ministries.
- Distribute fliers door-to-door. The most effective use of fliers involves personally inviting families at their door as the fliers are distributed. A team of fifteen can cover a fairly large subdivision in an evening or a Saturday morning.
- Publicize through pastors of sister churches.
- Put up signs.
- Concentrate on a number of evangelistic ministries: Child Evangelism classes, door-to-door witnessing, evangelistic movies (open air), an area-wide evangelistic meeting, evangelistic coffees, a teen coffee house, and others.
- Conduct a vacation Bible school.
- Use specialized ministries to meet people's needs: free or "partial-pay" legal services, counseling services, food assistance, clothing banks, mothers' clubs, mobile Christian library, and Saturday recreation groups.

- Make as many contacts as possible, by working through friends of people in the community, leaders of evangelistic ministries in the area, civic leaders, and social ministries (for example, Alcoholics Anonymous and the YMCA).

The pioneer church planter faces some major challenges in building a base for a new church. In the opinion of Galen Blom, an experienced church planter, "cold calling" is often not very fruitful, but wise networking can produce great opportunities for both evangelism and finding believers to join the new work. Blom suggests a four-part acrostic for effective networking: WEBB. (1) *W*eave your lives together relationally, finding common ground and shared passions. (2) *E*xpress vision and values clearly. (3) *B*elieve God is at work (testimonies and personal calling instill confidence that God is working). (4) *B*uild three levels of involvement (*players*, the core team; *participants*, both short-term and long-term; and *profit sharers*, believers willing to give to the project).[4]

Before beginning regular Sunday services, it is wise to gather the people who form the core for regular prayer and planning. It is also helpful to hold one or more home Bible classes in the community. This will accomplish three things: It will help draw committed Christians together, it will begin to develop the fellowship of the church, and it will provide evangelistic opportunities.

The seedling stage (regular Sunday services). Four basic challenges face the church-planting team at this point: finding a meeting place for Sunday services, appointing temporary leadership, securing the teaching and preaching staff, and appointing worship leaders and musicians.

Finding a *temporary meeting place* requires creativity. Here are a few suggestions: a public or private school, a college campus, a day-care center, a funeral home, a home, a union hall, a park recreation building, a community center, an apartment clubhouse, a gymnasium, a subdivision clubhouse, a mobile home, a portable building, a synagogue, an auto showroom, a bookstore, an office building, a tent, a hotel or motel, a courtroom.

A new church needs to find a meeting place that can be easily located by newcomers. It needs to be accessible, with sufficient parking, and it should provide a comfortable arrangement for regular church services as well as for small teaching groups. If at all possible, find a place that will allow you to have your own key. Also, before the first meeting, plan carefully for the care and cleanup of the rental facility. Go the "second mile" to maintain a good relationship with the landlord, to avoid damaging your testimony and hindering future church groups from renting the facility. For ideas on establishing a permanent location for a new church, see the section later in this chapter on "Buildings and Finances."

Once a church or group of Christians or an individual missionary is committed to the planting of a church, *core leaders* need to be found and authorized to proceed. The missionary or sponsoring church's board should appoint a temporary ministry committee (functioning as temporary elders) and a finance and facilities committee (functioning as temporary deacons). Permanent leaders should be ordained after a period of supervision by the home church. In the first few months it would be wise for the founding church or missionary to approve all new members and the selection of leaders.

Of major importance is the *selection of gifted preachers* to fill the pulpit of the new work. Until a pastor can be supported adequately, many interim possibilities may be available: gifted teachers in the mother church, staff members in the mother church, the senior pastor of the mother church (he could preach at an early service of the new work and then return to the home church for a later service, or vice versa), Bible college or seminary students from a nearby school, workers from local evangelical ministries, or a man added to the church staff for the purpose of starting churches.

Beginning a new church with *inspirational worship through music* will do much to propel the church forward. The music style needs to be chosen with the target group(s) in mind. For example, a church focusing on reaching Hispanics certainly needs to use instruments and music choices that fit the culture of that group. A ministry focused on people over fifty years of age will be quite different from one focused on people in their late twenties and thirties. The choice of music styles is important, but the "look" and "feel" of the service will also speak volumes to visitors.

The sapling stage. Within the first year the church needs to make solid progress toward becoming fully organized. Following are the key steps.

First, seek commitment by the core membership. For the first six to twelve months they should remain open to new people who would like to be a part of the charter membership. This will give a broader group a sense of ownership of the new church. Each person needs to be interviewed personally to be sure he or she knows Christ as Savior and agrees with the doctrine, organization, and philosophy of ministry of the new church. This will help avoid inroads of division in the church from the very beginning.

Second, gain a state charter. To receive tax-exempt status, a church needs to be registered as a nonprofit corporation. Neither a state charter nor tax-exempt status are a requirement to be a church, but obtaining both can protect members if they are audited by the Internal Revenue Service.

Third, acquire tax-exempt status (federal and state). After receiving the state's incorporation certificate, the church can then apply for tax-exempt status. National and state exemptions need to be applied for separately.

Since most of the support of a local church comes from people who expect to receive income-tax deductions for their contributions, it will be necessary at the beginning to channel all funds through the sponsoring church. As soon as possible, a lawyer should be contacted to arrange for a state, nonprofit corporation charter and a tax-exemption number.

Fourth, adopt a constitution, a doctrinal statment, and a policy statement. A church consitution and a doctrinal statement can be of great benefit to a church's stability. Church constitutions should normally be simple, short, and difficult to change.

Each church needs a short statement of faith on the basics of Christianity, which new members should be required to sign. A church also needs a more lengthy doctrinal statement that all elders and deacons should be required to sign and which teachers should be required to support in their teaching. Organizational details should appear in the church's policy statement, which can more readily be changed, if necessary, by a church board.

Fifth, select elders and deacons. This should be done cautiously. As stated earlier, new churches can function well with two temporary committees: a ministry committee and a facilities and finance committee. These two committees can do a lot of the work that normally would be done by elders and deacons. They should be appointed annually by the mother church or the church planter. It is normally wise to keep a mission church under the authority of the mother church until at least three elders surface as qualified leaders of the new church. Do not rush the appointment of leaders. One divisive leader can be devastating to a new church.

Sixth, call a pastor. A pastor should be selected with much prayer. Frequently church planters fall into two categories: the church-planting evangelist and the church-planting pastor. Sometimes it is wise to encourage the church-planting evangelist to move on after the first year or two and then call a church-planting pastor to establish and teach the church. If this arrangement is best for the church, it should be determined before the church is started. Some men, however, have multiple gifts and can fill both roles.

Steering Clear of Potential Problems

Doctrinal and philosophical issues. The New Testament places a high priority on the unity of the local church, as evidenced in almost every epistle. To prevent any major disunity in the future, the sponsoring church or church-planting missionary should write out clear objectives and plans for the new church well in advance of the first major meeting. The sponsoring church or church planter should, if possible, have a complete church constitution and doctrinal statement ready at that time.

Another way to prevent future problems is to know your beginning leaders well and to interview all charter members individually. Knowing of potential problem areas in advance is important. Common causes of division include the following positions and issues: the charismatic issue, extreme positions on church-government patterns, views concerning baptism and communion, legalistic views toward culturally related issues (for example, wearing hats to church, length of hair, etc.), following an outstanding Bible teacher, "double separation," and styles of worship.

Practical problems. It is helpful for the founding group to spend time fellowshipping together around the Word of God for a few months before establishing the church. This offers sufficient time to get to know each other well enough to minister together effectively. There are a few possible problems to guard against: Are there any in the group who are avid followers of any particular, well-known Bible teacher to the degree that they would not be teachable by other teachers? Is there any long-standing bitterness, resentment, or distrust among the core-group members? Are the founding members of the group motivated properly, or are they dominated by selfish motives or attitudes of reaction and criticism against other groups?

Care should also be taken to protect those handling the finances from suspicion. It is crucial to maintain good records of the church's income and expenses. Also it is wise to have each offering counted and deposited by two persons, not just one.

A good plan for dealing with any major future disagreements should also be included in the early business-meeting minutes of the church. Specific persons or groups (such as the church-planter missionary or the new church committee of the board in the mother church) should be designated as counselors, if difficulties arise.

Buildings and Finances

A permanent location. Determining a permanent location is, of course, a major decision the new church will have to make unless the mother church purchases the property in advance. (See also the discussion of facilities in chapter 8.)

Since new churches are usually limited financially, the following ideas might prove helpful:

- Obtain a long-term lease.
- Buy and build near compatible facilities such as a day-care center, a stadium parking lot, a shopping center that is closed on Sundays, a synagogue, a school, or a funeral home.
- Buy land in an area that needs a day-care center. Allow an investor to use your land for free to build a day-care center, in exchange for your use of the facility during the evenings and on weekends.
- Approach a developer of a new housing development about donating land for a new church.

Financing a new church. Obtaining sufficient finances to acquire a permanent facility can be a major challenge. Five major alternatives are open: (1) a gift or loan from the sponsoring church, (2) a gift or loan from a group of churches or a denomination, (3) a gift or loan from an independent Christian foundation or nonprofit corporation designed to channel gifts from individuals and churches to new works, (4) a loan from a secular institution, and (5) a bond program. If you pursue a bond issue, be sure to seek expert advice.

Leading a Church to Be Involved in Church Planting

Before you move into a church-planting program, you will probably need to convince the leaders and most of the church that the project is both important and realistic. You might think through your answers to possible spoken and unspoken objections, such as the following:

"It will hurt the home church." Some may be concerned that the home church might be hurt financially and spiritually through the loss of some of its members. However, this overlooks the sufficiency of God and the positive effect on the mother church of a vision for growth that church planting gives the congregation.

"The cost is too high; we can't afford it now." Examine what costs might be involved in planting a new church, and be ready to answer this question honestly and objectively.

"We will lose too many of our people and too much of our talent and leadership." Determine how many will be involved in the church plant, and who those people will be. Plan to encourage people in both the planting group and the mother church to use their talents. Usually church planting brings out dormant spiritual gifts of people who have been overlooked in the past.

"Our own ministry still has too many needs that should occupy the pastor's time and energy." A vision for fulfilling the Great Commission is the answer to this objection, but other practical questions also need to be addressed. What role will the pastor of the mother church play in the planting? Who else will help to provide leadership for the program?

"We shouldn't force a church on an area. We should wait until interested

people approach us from a specific area." There may be some validity to this objection, so carefully examine the specific area being considered for planting a new church. How will a new church help meet the spiritual needs of that area? What other churches are already there? Are they sound?

"*Another church nearby will impede the growth of our church.*" So long as the new church is not too close to the mother church, experience shows that just the opposite is true.

After you develop scriptural and practical replies to these questions, it would be wise to communicate these to the congregation in Sunday messages and church publications.

In bringing a church to being committed to planting a church the following steps are important:

- Be personally committed to the task and to God's timetable and direction.
- Pray regularly, and encourage other interested persons to join you in praying that the Lord will work in the hearts of your people.
- If you are the senior pastor, mention from the pulpit the scriptural mandate to develop churches and let the people know of your own personal burden.
- Discuss the idea with the more influential leaders of the church and ask them to pray with you about it.
- Plan ahead, and be prepared to furnish basic information on your suggestions to the leaders and the congregation.
- Get alone with the church leaders on a retreat to discuss the church's long-range plans. Bring up the subject of planting a church, along with a concrete proposal.
- Include church bulletin inserts in church planting (see three samples in Appendix C).
- Wait on the Lord. Don't become impatient and divide the church over the issue. Allow God time to work in people's hearts.

Launching and Maintaining a Movement

For church planting to become multiplication, it needs to be a movement; that is, the planted churches must themselves become planting churches. This can be facilitated in several ways. First, the church-planting agency or denomination can keep in contact with all churches in the association to encourage them and to cast the vision for multiplication. Second, the mother church's pastor and/or the church planter can speak often to the founding church leaders and pastor about the vision to multiply churches. Third, a group of churches interested in church planting can band together to form a fellowship of churches; then as each new church joins the fellowship it is challenged to support the ongoing church-planting efforts of the fellowship.

MULTIPLICATION THROUGH PASTORAL TRAINING IN THE CHURCH

Pastors and other church staff can appreciably expand their ability to multiply their ministries by joining with members, seminaries, and Bible schools in the process of training men for ministry. We often applaud the pastor who can develop men in his church to become church leaders because this helps multiply his ministry. The same is true of multiplying through the training of pastors for other churches.

The Role of the Local Church

In 1990, while I was serving as the president of Colorado Christian University in the Denver area, I began to discuss with Christian leaders ways to make the training of church leaders more effective. It became evident that traditional educational institutions (seminaries and colleges) were limited in their ability to provide students with adequate opportunities for spiritual growth and practical experience, while local churches seemed better equipped to do so.

My discussions with some of the staff of the Leadership Center at Dallas Seminary led to an invitation for me to participate in a meeting in Colorado Springs hosted by the Leadership Network (a Texas-based ministry with close ties to Dallas Seminary's Leadership Center).[5] The meeting included academic representatives of various evangelical seminaries and pastoral representatives from some megachurches that were developing their own "in-house" theological education programs. It seemed that a number of larger churches were becoming frustrated with the inability of many seminaries to provide adequate training for ministry.

As some evangelical seminaries have become more academically respectable, they have tended to lose touch with the world of ministry, and many of their graduates want to model their ministries after their professors, some of whom may have had limited pastoral experience. This may lead some people to conclude that seminary education may be good for producing more educators, but rather limited and sometimes counterproductive for producing effective evangelists, pastors, and missionaries.

However, to conclude that seminary education has no value would be shortsighted and foolish. Most churches are usually ill equipped to provide well-qualified scholars and high-quality resources (such as libraries).

The best solution, it seems, is to appropriate the strengths of both the seminaries and the local churches. In most cases the major share of the training in academic subjects such as Hebrew and Greek and much of the theological, biblical, and historical subjects should be done by seminaries. However, local churches should play a much larger role in the training of pastors and missionaries, and seminaries need to develop better ways to include local churches in the process.

Opportunities for Involvement

Many churches cooperate with seminaries and Bible colleges in the training of pastors by allowing students to carry out field-training assignments in the church. Other churches invite students to serve as interns for a summer or for a more extended period. Both methods can positively contribute to the training of Christian workers. However, an even greater partnership between schools and churches could yield larger dividends.

The Conservative Baptist Seminary of the East pioneered in developing partnerships with churches. This seminary originally was organized within churches in three locations: one in an urban environment (New York City), one in a suburban environment (Philadelphia), and one in a rural area (Connecticut). Each student was required to have a regular ministry in a church, and three mentors were assigned to each student: a professor, a pastor, and a businessman. The three mentors conferred regularly about the student's progress and they designed learning situations to help the student grow spiritually and in ministry skills. In several of the seminary's academic courses, assignments were given that related directly to each student's local-church ministry.

A similar partnership could be developed with more traditional seminaries. A church's pastor could be invited to assist a seminary's academic counselor in designing a course of study for a particular student. The student could be assigned to study at least one year in the partnering church. Courses could include practically oriented subjects such as pastoral ministry, missions, church planting and growth, evangelism, preaching, and the spiritual life, as well as some academic courses taught in the environment of practical application. For example, a pastor (working closely with an appointed faculty member) could lead the student in a study of Romans. Study assignments could be linked to ministry requirements such as having the student teach Romans in a Sunday-school class.

More and more seminaries are sensing the need for more practical training for ministry. Dallas Seminary, for example, has developed the "Barnabas Plan," in which students engage in ministry in a local church for a year and also gain credit for study in a field context. Such programs could be adapted and expanded to enhance the involvement of local churches in the training process. Whatever level of involvement is used, strategically minded pastors will include the training of future pastors as a part of their ministry plan.

MULTIPLICATION THROUGH EFFECTIVE MISSIONARY EFFORTS

Another way to apply the biblical principle of multiplication is through world missions. Participating in reaching unsaved people around the world with the gospel and in establishing local churches is an extremely effective and important part of any church-growth strategy for a church.

Our Changing World

In the past century the relationship between local churches and world missions has changed radically in at least five ways.

First, denominational missionary enterprises in the first half of this century were eclipsed by the rapid growth of faith missionary agencies. Faith missions served as interdenominational agencies, bringing together mission volunteers and financial support from churches both within and outside denominations. At the same time, the growth of the Bible college movement and evangelical seminaries provided a major impetus to the faith-missions movement.

Second, short-term missions became a major factor in world evangelization. Soon after the end of World War II, evangelistic parachurch ministries sprung up, such as the Navigators, Campus Crusade for Christ, and Overseas Christian Servicemen's Centers. These were soon followed by youth-captivating ministries like Youth with a Mission and Operation Mobilization. These ministries were structured to win people to Christ, disciple them, and then send them to serve both in America and around the world.

Local churches were called on to send their young people on short-term ministries overseas through these and other organizations. Soon members of church congregations were challenged to become personally involved in short-term projects. A few years ago, when the Berlin Wall came down and the door opened to the former Soviet Union and other Eastern European nations, mission organizations, schools, and churches united to move through that door with the largest cooperative short-term missions endeavor in history, called CoMission. Young people, business-men, housewives, and retirees responded to the challenge to serve in short-term missions assignments.

Third, during this century many mission fields have changed significantly. Although some fields remain virtually unreached, in a number of countries indigenous churches have their own national leaders, and some now have become "missionary-sending" national churches.

Fourth, the world has changed. Many nations that were closed to any gospel witness have become more open. The world has become a smaller place through revolutionary changes in transportation and communication. At the same time Western democracies have become much more affluent.

Fifth, many people from Third-World countries now reside in Western countries. Muslim mosques and Hindu temples have been built in many major American and British cities. This has placed the mission field at our doorstep.

Opportunities for Involvement

Local churches can now become more directly involved in world missions than ever before. In addition to supporting world missions by sending our young people and supplying financial support, more local-church people can now become personally involved in missions. Adults can engage in overseas short-term mission projects for one or more weeks, or even a summer or an entire year. Transportation is relatively cheap, and most places in the world are fairly easy to get to. Communication by telephone, fax, and e-mail makes it easier than in the past for churches to keep in touch with their people serving in most places in the world.

Inadequate Responses

The Christian community needs to respond quickly and wisely to these changes. However, some churches may be missing remarkable opportunities for making a major impact for Christ overseas.

Unfortunately some pastors, sensing that some mission fields no longer need the same kind of missionary involvement, have reduced or even discontinued their missions program and budget. Others continue with business as usual, supporting traditional missionary strategies that may not be effective. Still others become so enamored with exposing their people to the needs of the world that they send so many short-term missionaries that they actually become a burden to career missionaries and national churches.

The Response of the Wise Visionary

Vision and wisdom are essential if your church is to have an effective missionary impact. To help your church have an effective missions program, consider the following suggestions:

- As outlined in Acts 1:8 develop an evangelistic strategy to reach your

"Jerusalem," your immediate community of a similar race and culture as your church. Then plan to reach out across cultural and racial boundaries into a neighboring region. Include plans for involving your church in inner-city ministries. Then get involved in the evangelization of the lost and the planting of churches in countries around the world.

- Emphasize both pioneer work among unreached peoples (Rom. 15:20) and praying for laborers to enter fields where the harvest is ripe (Matt. 9:37–38; John 4:35).
- Focus on these key elements in your missions emphasis: evangelism and follow-up of new believers, church planting, helping local churches grow, and training church leaders.
- Encourage cooperation between mission agencies so as to enhance their effectiveness.
- Develop a strategy that helps national churches become completely independent of foreign control or support as quickly as possible. Sending missionaries to countries with a strong growing national church should be done carefully. Missionaries from outside the country should have special expertise that the national church does not yet have, such as seminary-trained teachers and people with technical expertise.
- Ask the missionaries your church supports to give you an annual report so you can assess their effectiveness.

A good example of the application of these principles took place recently among a group of pastors in Texas. They teamed up with two missionary agencies (East-West Ministries and Campus Crusade for Christ) and some Canadian churches to try to reach five Muslim-dominated countries in Central Asia. The ethnic populations (Kazakhs, Uzbeks, Turkmen, Kyrgyz, and Tadjiks) of these former Soviet republics were virtually unreached for Christ. A small team of Western missionaries formed a small Bible school and training center, with a one-year curriculum, called the Central Asia Leadership Training Center (CALTC) with the assistance of young Russian-speaking nationals from Kazakhstan. Pastors from the North American churches did much of the teaching. By the end of three years the school had planted sixteen churches throughout the five Muslim-dominated republics. All the churches were started and pastored by nationals, and most of the school's leadership responsibilities had been transferred to nationals with some Western assistance. Each year the pastors of the supporting churches travel to Central Asia to teach. Also they meet together once a year in the States to evaluate the program and to pray for each church planter.

CONCLUSION

What a thrill to be a part of church growth by multiplication! Most churches of any size can multiply their effectiveness by participating in planting a new church, helping train future pastors, and being involved in a variety of missionary efforts.

Biblically, church growth should be both qualitative and quantitative—and in that order. The qualitative dimensions are absolute and are applicable no matter what the numerical potential in a given environment. The quantitative dimensions should be related to the population in any given community.

When we keep this sequence in focus, we can help a church grow biblically. If we do not, we will be tempted to allow culture and pragmatics to drive our thinking and planning. Furthermore, we'll discourage pastors who are laboring in communities where numerical growth is limited because of environmental factors. Hopefully, this book will help all of us to maintain proper biblical priorities and God-designed balances.

Appendix A

A Suggested Model for a Healthy Church Plant

One mission organization has developed the following description of churches they encourage nationals to plant in the former Soviet Union.[1]

Beliefs

1. Biblically based evangelical theology
2. A clear gospel of grace (salvation through faith, not works)
3. Grace teaching (freedom in Christ to live a life of holy commitment to Christ, looking to Jesus and the judgment seat of Christ)
4. The believer's spiritual growth, dependent on a clear understanding of his assurance of salvation
5. The autonomy of the local church and the leadership by a plurality of leaders
6. A biblical realism about life (with its struggles and suffering) as strangers and pilgrims in a fallen world
7. Spiritual warfare and victory through Christ, and the need for separation from the materialism and selfish ambition

Practices

1. Baptism of believers by immersion
2. The Lord's Supper as a symbolic memorial of Christ's death
3. Regular worship and prayer of the church body

4. Discipling, maturing, and equipping of all believers for the work of the ministry
5. All believers growing in sacrificial giving to the church, other ministries, and other believers in need
6. All believers involved in ministering to others in the church fellowship
7. Meeting various needs of church members
8. Evangelistic outreach of the church as a whole and of all the members individually
9. Support of missionaries and missionary works
10. The expression of Christ's love by the church in ministering to those in need in the community

Operational Principles or Characteristics

1. Teaches and promotes the ministry of the Holy Spirit and prayer in leadership decisions and in the lives and ministries of every member of the church
2. Clearly articulates a biblically based mission and goals, including a visionary recognition of God's primary target area(s) for the church's ministry
3. Has Spirit-led, relevant, expository preaching
4. Is self-supporting and is managed well with integrity, wise organization, and good records
5. Is committed to church growth and the multiplication of churches
6. Attempts to motivate and train every person in the congregation to participate in ministry and maintain winsome involvement with unbelievers as a basis for evangelism
7. Is sensitive to the needs and interests of the unchurched in its signs, friendliness, services, and outreach events and programs
8. Develops and multiplies spiritual, visionary leaders who are regularly discipling others
9. Ministers to the needs of families, children, and young people, recognizing the special needs of spiritually mixed marriages and single parents
10. Develops and multiplies small groups through which spiritual growth, fellowship, prayer, and evangelism can be carried on

Appendix B

Guidelines for What to Teach in a New Church

During the early stages of the formation of a new church the pastor or church planter needs to present studies and sermons on these crucial, foundational topics:

1. The elements of a balanced, healthy church (teaching, fellowship, worship and prayer, and outreach) and how the planned church will be organized.
2. Basic doctrines, including the gospel, the person of Christ, the Trinity, the nature of the Scriptures, grace, the ministry of the Holy Spirit, and the nature of the church
3. Principles for living the Spirit-filled life in our relationships with each other
4. Lifestyle evangelism
5. What a healthy Christian home looks like

Also the leaders need to study the role of the pastor, how to call a pastor, and elder qualifications.

Appendix C

FIRST SAMPLE

What Is a Mission Church?

- It is a new church, an infant church, a new assembly of believers.
- It is a part of God's plan for fulfilling the Great Commission.
- It is an essential ingredient in world evangelism.
- It is another center for evangelistic outreach.
- It is another center for family worship, study, growth, and service.
- It is another base for sending God's missionary servants to the ends of the earth.
- It is another base for Christ-centered activities for young people and children.
- It is an exciting opportunity for spiritual growth in the "mother" church as it assists in giving birth to a new church.
- It is a significant means for bringing the Word of God to the people of a given community.

SECOND SAMPLE

Why Establish Mission Churches in Our Area?

- Our area is growing at a rate that exceeds the population explosion in our nation.

- More doctrinally sound churches are needed in our area.
- A strong Bible-teaching ministry is essential to the spiritual growth of the many new converts in our area.
- The closer a church is to the people, the more they will become involved in the ministry of the church.
- A mission church offers one of the most effective means of long-range multiplication.
- Because of the urgency of the hour, we need to use every means available for the building up of the church of the Lord Jesus Christ.

THIRD SAMPLE

How Can Each of Us Participate in Starting a New Church?

- By praying, both individually and in groups
- By assisting in the new church's worship services, through music, leading in prayer, and other means
- By assisting in the Sunday school when it is established
- By canvassing the area
- By helping in the distribution of advertising literature
- By assisting with weekday Bible classes
- By being available for consultation as elders, treasurer, Sunday school superintendent, deacons, committees, boys- and girls-club leaders, and others
- By occasional joint fellowship meetings with the new church
- By giving financially to help support the new work

Appendix D

Biblical Principles of Church Government

THE PURPOSE OF CHURCH GOVERNMENT

The purpose of church organization is to furnish the best workable structure that will help the church follow the leadership of Christ and will facilitate the most effective implementation of the church's ministries

CHURCH GOVERNMENT AND THE ISSUE OF FORM AND FUNCTION

In the area of church government the New Testament emphasizes purpose, principle, and function, not particular forms and practices. Precise and absolute forms and procedures were not given to the church in the New Testament, in contrast to the explicit forms and procedures for Israel in the Old Testament. The absence of any clear, detailed instructions for church government and the emphasis on church behavior and relationships further confirm the relative freedom churches may have in form, organization, and government. Each function should be based on purpose-oriented principles. Following is a brief list of New Testament church- government patterns, followed by the principles that seem to be implied.

NEW TESTAMENT PATTERNS AND PRINCIPLES FOR CHURCH GOVERNMENT

(1) Structure

Pattern: In the New Testament churches elders ruled (1 Tim. 5:17; Heb. 13:17; 1 Pet. 5:5), deacons served, and teachers and pastor-teachers exercised their gifts with authority (1 Pet. 4:11). All leaders were expected to minister with servant attitudes (1 Cor. 4:1; 2 Tim. 2:24–25; 1 Pet. 5:3–6). The local church normally exercised authority corporately in major issues (Matt. 18:16–17; Acts 11:22; 15:22; 1 Cor. 5:4–5; 2 Cor. 8:19).

Principle: The mature leaders were publicly recognized and followed, though the church was responsible to participate with the leaders in major decisions and could remove elders through church discipline, if necessary. Special needs were met by specially selected servant-managers called deacons. God's gifted teachers were recognized and allowed to teach the Scriptures authoritatively.

(2) Relation to Other Church Bodies

Pattern: No organization of churches existed above the local churches, but fellowship between churches was encouraged, including financial aid and cooperative decisions relating to church testimony (Acts 15; 2 Cor. 8:9).

Principle: Local churches were autonomous, and yet there was cooperation between church bodies.

(3) Congregational Responsibility

Pattern: The entire local church had responsibility (and authority) in the two areas of maintaining doctrinal purity (2 Cor. 11:4), and removing members from the fellowship (Matt. 18:16–17; 1 Cor. 5:4–5; 2 Cor. 2; 1 Tim. 5:17–20). Furthermore believers participated in decisions related to other major matters: selecting the two nominees for an apostle to replace Judas (Acts 1:15–23), selecting the deacon prototypes (6:1–8), and sending emissaries to check on the new church at Antioch (11:19–23).

Principle: Part of the responsibility for the purity of the church membership and leaders rests with the congregation.

(4) Church Membership

Pattern: The Scriptures include five qualifications necessary for a person to be recognized as a part of a local congregation: saved (Acts 2:47; 5:14), baptized (2:41; 10:47), in doctrinal agreement on major issues (Gal. 1:9), submissive to the leaders of the congregation (1 Thess. 5:14; 2 Thess. 3:4, 14; Heb. 13:7, 17, 24), and morally pure (1 Cor. 5:1–5, 13; 2 Cor. 7:1; 1 Thess. 4:3).

Principle: It is necessary to clarify who constitutes the church (members) in order for the church to carry out its responsibilities.

(5) Elders and Pastors

Pattern: The New Testament provides much helpful information about the leaders of local churches.

1. Titles: The titles for church leaders were "elder" (Greek, *presbuteros*) and "overseer" (Greek, *episkopos*), and, though not every elder possessed the gift of pastor, their job was to pastor or shepherd (Greek, *poimainō*) the church (see Acts 20:17, 28; Titus 1:5–7; 1 Pet. 5:1–2).

2. Plurality of elders: Unless referred to generically, elders for a given local church were always spoken of in the plural (Acts 20:17; Phil. 1:1).

3. Pastors and teachers: The terms *pastor* and *teacher* (and the implied pastor-teacher) referred to the spiritually gifted people given to the church to fill the roles of pastoring and teaching the church (Eph. 4:11). The terms were not necessarily titles for church officers, but were positions of ministry. At least one church seems to have had a team of pastors and teachers and prophets providing special leadership (Acts 13:1–3), and Paul indicated that churches should provide financial support for leaders who minister God's Word (1 Cor. 9:7–14; 1 Tim. 5:17–18).

4. Selection of elders: The elders were publicly recognized by the apostles

or apostolic representatives (Acts 14:23; 1 Tim. 5:22). We have no one with apostolic authority today. The only possible parallel would be a missionary church planter or the elders of a mother church, who would recognize the first group of elders in a new local church.

5. Qualifications of elders: The qualifications for elders are listed in 1 Timothy 3:2–7 and Titus 1:6–9. These were the observable characteristics of a mature believer. They may be understood as attainable qualities that any man (no matter what sins or failures characterized his past) could reach by God's grace. The Scriptures indicate that elders need not be appointed until qualified men are available or have been developed. The church at Corinth apparently had no elders, just outstanding teachers, and Paul warned against too quickly appointing anyone as a leader (1 Tim. 5:22).

6. Tenure of the elders: The Scriptures are silent on this issue, except for the possible parallel with the synagogue. In the Jewish community the elders of the community of the faithful in any given location were recognized as mature leaders, apparently for life. The emphasis on qualifications and the lack of any mention of term of office in the Scriptures also tends to support the view that elders were appointed for life or until they ceased to function as elders.

7. Responsibilities of the elders: Elders' responsibilities are found in various parts of the New Testament:
   - Oversee or manage; giving direction to the entire ministry (the title "overseer" implies this; 1 Tim. 3:1).
   - Rule; directing all the affairs of the church, under the authority of Christ (Acts 20:28; 1 Tim. 5:17; Heb. 13:17; 1 Pet. 5:5).
   - Be an example (1 Pet. 5:3).
   - Lead without lording it over the flock (1 Pet. 5:3).
   - Guard the flock (Acts 20:28) and refute false teachers (Titus 1:9).
   - Pastor or care for the needs of the flock (Acts 20:28).
   - Provide for the spiritual feeding of the flock (Acts 20:28).
   - Teach and exhort (1 Tim. 3:2; Titus 1:9; Heb. 13:7).
   - Pray for the sick, and anoint with oil if requested (James 5:13–15).

Principles: These patterns can be summarized under the following principle.

First, the major leaders of the church are the elders (normally more than one), who may include a teaching staff (one or more). A church can function for a time without elders or without a specially called teaching staff, but it is healthiest with both.

Second, the Scriptures do not state how elders are to be selected. But since a church is to follow leaders who meet specific qualifications, the congregation must be involved in selecting its elders. However, in view of 1 Timothy 5:22 elder selection must also include their being recognized by existing mature church leaders. In a new work the elders of a mother or sister church or a church planter can function in this capacity.

Third, a church needs to emphasize the importance of spiritual maturity in the men who serve as elders.

Fourth, the elders are obviously to rule, but elder rule does not mean they can lord it over the flock, nor does it exclude the congregation from recognizing God's qualified leaders. Balance is to be maintained between some aspects of congregational government and elder rule.

Fifth, the church structure and ministry should be arranged so that the elders not only govern the church but also minister to the needs of the people.

(6) Deacons

Pattern: The biblical data concerning deacons is somewhat limited, probably because the role of deacons was to be flexible so that a church could adapt to changes in its needs.

1. Role: To serve in the places the leaders (elders) deemed necessary (indicated by the meaning of the term "deacon" and by the example of the deacon prototypes in Acts 6).
2. Selection: Recommended by the congregation and confirmed by the elders (Acts 6).
3. Tenure: Not stated in Scripture.
4. Qualifications: Listed in 1 Timothy 3:8–12.
5. Deaconesses: Some Bible students believe that women served as deaconesses (Rom. 16:1; 1 Tim. 3:11).

Principle: When the church leaders (elders) recognize a particular need (for example, care for the poor, finances, facilities), then they should ask the congregation to recommend Spirit-filled men and/or women for those job(s). The elders should make the final decision as to whether the persons are spiritually qualified and then publicly recognize them as deacons and/or deaconesses.

(7) Finances

Pattern: The New Testament epistles give some important guidelines for the church's operation and approach to giving.

1. Tithing is not mentioned in the epistles.
2. Giving first involved giving oneself to the Lord (2 Cor. 8:5).
3. Collections were to come under the oversight of the church leaders (Acts 4:35; 11:29–30).
4. Care was taken to avoid misuse of funds and to keep the church blameless in the use of finances (2 Cor. 8:19–20).
5. Churches made pledges and were expected to keep their pledges by taking regular offerings (8:9).

Principle: Church leaders are not to use pressure or manipulation in asking the congregation to give, but are to teach the biblical principles of giving. The elders are responsible for overseeing the collection and disbursement of the church's funds.

Appendix E

A Sample Church Constitution

In the process of planting a church the church-planting team needs to focus on evangelism and people relations. So it may prove helpful to borrow documents from other sources. Following is a sample constitution that the organizing team could adapt to its needs. It is wise to keep the church constitution as brief as possible and to put details of church organization and procedures in a policy manual that can be modified, when necessary, by the elders.

PREAMBLE

To the glory of God, the _____ Church is established to carry out the following four God-ordained functions.

1. Teaching—to stand for the historic, fundamental, Christian truths, and to equip the saints for the work of service, for the building up of the body of Christ; with the goal of attaining unity, knowledge of the Son of God, and the maturity that is measured by the fullness of Christ.

2. Fellowship—to provide a means of developing meaningful fellowship among believers: caring for and loving one another, warning, stimulating, and encouraging each other to lead healthy spiritual lives.

3. Outreach—to participate in evangelism in the local community and around the world, and to encourage and train God's people to

have an effective influence and loving ministry in various contexts.

4. Worship and prayer—to provide for meaningful worship and prayer, and to administer the ordinances of water baptism and the Lord's Supper.

ARTICLE I: NAME

The name of this church shall be the _____ Church of the city of _____, State of _____, a __(state)_____ corporation having its principal place of worship at _____, hereinafter referred to as "the church."

This corporation is a nonprofit Christian organization established for the purposes as set forth in the preamble hereof. The term for which this corporation is to exist is perpetual. In the event of dissolution of said corporation, all assets, revenues, proceeds, and funds from whatever source, must be distributed to organizations whose convictions are similar to those set forth in the preamble.

ARTICLE II: DOCTRINE

Section 1: The Importance of Doctrine

This church shall function as a _____ church committed to the Christian truths recorded in God's inerrant written revelation, the Holy Scriptures. All elders, ministerial staff, and regular teachers must wholeheartedly agree with the Articles of Faith (Section 2 of this article) and the Doctrinal Statement (attached to and considered a part of this constitution). Also all members must be in full agreement with the Articles of Faith.

Section 2: Articles of Faith

    A. The Trinity: God exists in three, eternal, coequal persons, the Father, the Son, and the Holy Spirit.

B. The person of Christ: Undiminished deity (true God) and complete humanity are united forever in one, sinless, virgin-born person, the Lord Jesus Christ.

C. The work of Christ: The death of Christ served as a perfect, God-satisfying, substitute payment of the penalty for the sins of the world. His bodily resurrection guarantees eternal life for all who believe in Him.

D. Personal salvation: One can be assured of God's forgiveness and deliverance from eternal separation from God in hell and receive the sure hope of eternal life only through personal trust in the Lord Jesus Christ and acceptance of God's free gift of life through Christ.

E. Revelation: God has revealed Himself and His will through the divinely inspired Scriptures.

ARTICLE III: GOVERNMENT

Section 1: Authority and Responsibility

A. The ultimate authority for the leadership of this church resides in the head of the church, the Lord Jesus Christ. For purposes of implementing our Lord's will in the life of this church, the church as a body (the congregation) shall have the responsibility to recognize qualified men in the church as elders, and to submit to their leadership. All ministries and activities of the church shall function under the authority of the elders, and the elders (or those to whom the elders delegate authority) shall determine all church policies and procedures.

B. The elders must have the approval of a majority of the congregation (in a properly called congregational business meeting) for the following major decisions: the selection of elders and the senior pastor, the purchase of property, and major construction of new buildings.

Section 2: Membership

A. Procedure for joining the membership of the church shall be determined by the elders.
B. Qualifications for membership include the following:
    1. Profession of faith in Christ.
    2. Believer's baptism (immersion shall be encouraged, though not required of believers coming from another church: however, the normal practice of this church shall be immersion).
    3. Willingness to submit to the elders of this church.
    4. Agreement with the Articles of Faith of the church and a commitment not to propagate any doctrine contrary to the attached Doctrinal Statement.
C. Discipline and dismissal of members: The elders shall establish procedures for discipline and dismissal of members in accord with biblical guidelines.

Section 3: Leadership

A. Elders: The church shall recognize men to serve as elders who meet the qualifications of 1 Timothy 3:2–7 and Titus 1:6–9. The selection of new elders requires approval by three-fourths of all active elders and two-thirds of the congregation in a properly called business meeting. Elders may continue to serve as elders so long as they remain biblically qualified and are actively engaged in providing leadership and shepherding to the church. The removal of an elder from his position as an elder requires a unanimous vote of the other elders or a two-thirds vote of the congregation. The elders shall annually elect their chairman and other officers as determined by the elders, by majority vote.
B. Church staff: The staff of the church shall consist of the senior pastor and other staff members determined by the elders. The senior pastor shall have the oversight of other staff members and shall have the authority to employ and dismiss staff members with the advice and consent of the elders, or an approved committee of the elders.

The elders shall determine all other responsibilities and authority of the senior pastor, who shall also be recognized as an elder. The senior pastor may be dismissed by a unanimous vote of the elders or a two-thirds vote of both the elders and the congregation.

C. Deacons: The elders may appoint deacons and/or deaconesses to manage specific areas of responsibility. The elders shall determine the selection procedure and their term of office. The procedure shall include an opportunity for the congregation to make recommendations to the elders of Spirit-filled men and women.

D. Treasurer: The elders shall appoint a deacon to serve as treasurer, whose responsibilities shall include the supervising of the collection, deposit, and disbursement of all funds, the keeping of the church's financial records, and the providing of financial reports to the elders and congregation as required by the elders.

Section 3: Business Meetings

A. Elder business meetings: All elders must be notified in a timely fashion of all elder meetings. A 60 percent attendance is required for a quorum in all elder meetings. All decisions (unless otherwise indicated in this constitution) shall require a majority of all in attendance for approval. However, the elders shall prayerfully attempt to achieve unanimity on all major decisions.

B. Congregational business meetings: The senior pastor, the chairman of the elders, any three elders, or 5 percent of the active membership of the church (in a written petition), may call a congregational business meeting. All meetings must be announced at least one week in advance and must include a public announcement in the Sunday morning service (or services, if more than one Sunday morning service is regularly scheduled). Those in attendance shall constitute a quorum. The chairman of the elders or his designate shall chair all congregational business meetings. The elders may also use a written ballot or poll of the congregation in the Sunday morning service(s) in lieu of a meeting.

ARTICLE IV: AMENDMENTS

This constitution may be revised or amended by a two-thirds vote of the elders and a majority vote of the congregation in a properly called business meeting.

ADDENDUM

Until the church has at least three qualified elders, the elders of the mother church shall have authority over the church, appointing temporary church leaders as deemed appropriate. Elders of the mother church must approve all new elders until the church has three elders. If there is no mother church, the church-planting pastor shall have the authority to lead the church in the place of elders.

Appendix F

Evaluating the Three Vital Experiences in a Church

The following questions are based on the Jerusalem model recorded in Acts 2:12–47 (see chapter 4).

Learning Experiences with the Word of God

- Do the forms and structures of our church allow for a balance in learning the Word of God, in having relational experiences with one another and with God, and in sharing Christ with others?

  Unsatisfactory   1   2   3   4   5   Satisfactory

- Is the Word of God taught clearly and regularly?

  Unsatisfactory   1   2   3   4   5   Satisfactory

  a. Is the Word of God taught with variety (for example, verse-by-verse, topical studies, biographical studies) without being "locked in" to one particular approach?

  Unsatisfactory   1   2   3   4   5   Satisfactory

b. Is there a good balance between teaching from the Old Testament and the New Testament?

Unsatisfactory   1   2   3   4   5   Satisfactory

c. Is the Word of God applied to present-day living?

Unsatisfactory   1   2   3   4   5   Satisfactory

d. Are people learning how to study the Word of God on their own?

Unsatisfactory   1   2   3   4   5   Satisfactory

Relational Experiences with One Another and with God

- Do our structures allow for relationships with God to grow naturally out of relationships with people?

Unsatisfactory   1   2   3   4   5   Satisfactory

a. Do our structures and approaches allow for the Lord's Supper to be a meaningful experience, involving deep relationships with people?

Unsatisfactory   1   2   3   4   5   Satisfactory

b. Is prayer vital and dynamic, based on an awareness of human needs in the church, or are we locked into traditional approaches to prayer that make it nonpersonal, nebulous, general, and meaningless?

Unsatisfactory   1   2   3   4   5   Satisfactory

c. Is giving spontaneous, regular, and joyful in the context of meeting the needs of people? Or is giving a mechanical process that we are expected to engage in, without knowing what the needs are for which we are giving or how the money is used?

Unsatisfactory   1   2   3   4   5   Satisfactory

d. Does our music represent a balance between songs and hymns that teach and admonish one another and those that exalt and glorify God? Do we have freedom to use music that is expressed in various ways, or are we limited to music that we are culturally conditioned to accept and appreciate?

Unsatisfactory   1   2   3   4   5   Satisfactory

Witnessing Experiences with the Unsaved World

- Do our structures allow opportunities for our people to share Christ with others? Or are people so busy attending church meetings that they don't have time to build bridges with non-Christians and to share Christ with them?

Unsatisfactory   1   2   3   4   5   Satisfactory

- Do we have time to relate to Christians who are not members of our church—in our homes, in recreational settings, and in informal settings? Or do our relationships with people consist only of attending meetings together, sitting in long rows, and listening to someone talk to us?

Unsatisfactory   1   2   3   4   5   Satisfactory

Endnotes

CHAPTER 1
THINKING BIBLICALLY ABOUT CHURCH GROWTH

1. *Disciple* or *disciples,* as a synonym for *Christian(s),* occurs in these verses in Acts: 6:1, 2, 7; 9:1, 10, 19, 26 (twice), 36, 38; 2:26, 29; 13:52; 14:20, 22, 28: 15:10; 16:1; 18:23, 27; 19:9, 30; 20:1, 21:4, 16 (twice). And a number of times in Acts the Greek word for "brothers" *(adelphoi)* is used of Christians: 1:15–16; 2:27; 6:3; 11:1; 12:29; 14:2; 15:3, 22, 32, 36, 40; 16:2, 40; 17:10, 14; 18:18, 27; 21:7, 17; 28:14–15, 21.

CHAPTER 2
A THREE-LENS PARADIGM

1. Alvin Tofler, *Future Shock* (New York: Random House, 1970).
2. Alvin Tofler, *Third Wave* (New York: Bantam Books, 1980).

CHAPTER 4
THREE VITAL EXPERIENCES

1. R. S. Wallace, "Lord's Supper," in *International Standard Bible Encyclopedia,* ed. Geoffrey W. Bromiley (Grand Rapids: Eerdmans, 1986), 3:167.

CHAPTER 6
THE FOUNDATIONS FOR EVANGELISM AND MISSIONS

1. Merrill C. Tenney, *John: The Gospel of Belief* (Grand Rapids: Eerdmans, 1953), 199.
2. Francis Schaeffer, *The Church at the End of the Twentieth Century* (Downers Grove, Ill.: InterVarsity, 1970), 139.

CHAPTER 7
GOD'S PLAN FOR CHURCH LEADERSHIP

1. M. H. Shepherd, Jr., "Bishop," in *Interpreter's Dictionary of the Bible,* ed. George A. Buttrick (Nashville: Abingdon, 1962), 1:442.
2. H. E. Dosker, "Bishop," in *International Standard Bible Encyclopedia,* 1 (1979): 516.

CHAPTER 8
GROWTH STRATEGIES WITHIN THE LOCAL CHURCH

1. Christian A. Schwarz, *Natural Church Development* (Carol Stream, Ill.: ChurchSmart Resources, 1996).
2. Ibid., 14.
3. Ibid., 16.
4. Ibid., 20.
5. Ibid., 23
6. Ibid., 23.
7. Ibid., 24.
8. Ibid., 25.
9. Ibid., 26.
10. Ibid., 27.
11. Bill Bright, discussion with leaders of Campus Crusade for Christ, Fort Collins, Colorado, July 1994.
12. Glenn S. Martin and Gary L. McIntosh, "Prayer in Changing Times: Part One," *McIntosh Church Growth Network*, June 1992, 1.
13. Ibid., 1–2.

14. Glenn S. Martin and Gary L. McIntosh, "Prayer in Changing times: Part Two," *McIntosh Church Growth Network,* July 1992, 1–2.

15. Schwarz, *Natural Church Development,* 28–29.

16. See Lucy Mabery-Foster, *Women and the Church,* Swindoll Leadership Library (Nashville: Word, 1999) for creative ways to minister to women today.

17. Schwarz, *Natural Church Development,* 30–31.

18. Ibid., 32.

19. Ibid., 34-35.

20. Ibid., 36–37.

21. Ibid., 42.

22. Ibid., 42.

23. Ibid., 46-48.

24. Robert E. Logan, *Beyond Church Growth* (Old Tappan, N.J.: Revell, 1989), ???

25. Timothy Hawks, telephone conversation with author, Joe L. Wall, Austin, Texas, October 1997.

26. Timothy Hawks (Austin, Tex.: unpublished notes, n.d.).

27. Aubrey Malphurs, *Planting Growing Churches for the Twenty-first Century* (Grand Rapids: Baker, 1992), 168–71.

CHAPTER 9
CHURCH GROWTH BY MULTIPLICATIONS

1. Robert E. Logan and Steven L. Ogne, The Church Planter's Toolkit (Carol Stream, Ill.: ChurchSmart Resources, 1994), 4:3.

2. In the 1970s the Spring Branch Community Church of Houston, Texas, and its pastors started a church-planting multiplication process that resulted in the establishing of more than twenty churches.

3. Logan and Ogne, *The Church Planter's Toolkit,* ???.

4. Galen Blom (unpublished notes, 1998).

5. Leadership Network, 2501 Cedar Springs Road, Suite 200, Dallas Texas 75201.

APPENDIX A
A SUGGESTED MODEL FOR A HEALTHY CHURCH PLANT

1. East-West Ministries International, Houston, Texas.

Bibliography

Anderson, Leith. *A Church for the Twenty-first Century*. Minneapolis: Bethany House Publishers, 1992.

Barna, George. *User-Friendly Churches*. Ventura, Calif.: Regal Books, 1991.

Becker, Paul. *Dynamic Church Planting*. Vista, Calif.: Multiplication Ministries, 1992.

Easum, William M. *The Church Growth Handbook*. Nashville: Abingdon Press, 1990.

Hemphill, Ken. *The Antioch Effect: Eight Characteristics of Highly Effective Churches*. Nashville: Broadman and Holman Publishers, 1994.

Jenson, Ron, and Jim Stevens. *Dynamics of Church Growth*. Grand Rapids: Baker Book House, 1981.

Lawrence, William D. *Effective Pastoring*. Swindoll Leadership Library. Nashville: Word Publishing, 1999.

Logan, Robert E. *Beyond Church Growth*. Old Tappan, N.J.: Fleming H. Revell Co., 1989.

————, and Steven L. Ogne. *The Church Planter's Toolkit*. Carol Stream, Ill.: ChurchSmart Resources, 1994.

Malphurs, Aubrey. *Planting Growing Churches for the Twenty-First Century*. Grand Rapids: Baker Book House, 1992.

McGavran, Donald A. *Understanding Church Growth*. 3d. ed. Revised and edited by C. Peter Wagner. Grand Rapids: Wm. B. Eerdmans Publishing Co., 1990.

McIntosh, Gary, and Glenn Martin. *Finding Them, Keeping Them: Effective Strategies for Evangelism and Assimilation in the Local Church*. Nashville: Broadman Press, 1992.

Petersen, Jim. *Church without Walls*. Colorado Springs: Navpress, 1992.

Rainer, Thom S. *The Book of Church Growth: History, Theology, and Principles*. Nashville: Broadman and Holman Publishers, 1993.

———. *Eating the Elephant. Bite-Sized Steps to Achieve Long-Term Growth in Your Church*. Nashville: Broadman and Holman Publishers, 1994.

Schwarz, Christian A. *Natural Church Development*. Carol Stream, Ill.: ChurchSmart Resources, 1996.

Steffen, Tom A. *Passing the Baton: Church Planting That Empowers*. La Habra, Calif.: Center of Organizational and Ministry Development, 1993.

Taylor, Richard S. *Dimensions of Church Growth*. Grand Rapids: Zondervan Publishing House, 1989.

Towns, Elmer L., John N. Vaughan, and David J. Seifert. *The Complete Book of Church Growth*. 2d ed. Wheaton, Ill.: Tyndale House Publishers, 1990.

Wagner, C. Peter. *Leading Your Church to Growth*. Ventura, Calif.: Regal Books, 1984.

———. *The Healthy Church*. Ventura, Calif.: Regal Books, 1996.

Warren, Rick. *The Purpose Driven Church*. Grand Rapids: Zondervan Publishing House, 1995.

Scripture Index

Subject Index

judgment seat of Christ, 9
Upper Room discourse, 71–74
vineyard analogy, 74–76.
See also Spiritual growth; Spiritual
   maturity
Jethro, 98
Joab, 19
John Mark, 21
Judas, 74–75
Kingdom
   and church growth strategies, 5–10
   as present and future, 7–8
   in New Testament, 7–8
   in Old Testament, 6.
   Jesus Christ as Son of David, 11–12
   making disciples, 13–14
   See also Church planting

—L—

Last Supper. *See* Lord's Supper
Lazarus, 78
Leadership, 83–93
   core leaders for new church, 128
   empowering the congregation, 98–99
   need for visionary leaders, 108
   servant leadership, 93.
   See also Elders
Leadership Center, 134
Leadership Network, 134
Leading Your Church to Grow, 95
Liturgical services, 103
Local church
   and God's plan for salvation, 77–81
   as family, 85–86
   as focus of church growth, 35–36
   biblically healthy church, 107–10
   evaluation of programs.
      See Appendix F
   in New Testament, 16–17, 36–42, 77
   member participation, 57–69
   need for balance, 53–55
   qualities of growing church, 96–107
   role in pastoral training, 134–35
   staff duties, 86–87

world mission opportunities, 138–39.
   See also Cell church model; Church;
      Church growth; Church planting;
      Elders; Finances; House churches;
      Love; Leadership; Members;
      Prayer; Spiritual growth; Spiritual
      maturity; Witnessing; Worship
Location, 115–16
Logan, Robert, 95, 108, 123
Lord's Supper
   and spiritual maturity, 46–48.
   See also Upper Room
Love, 36–42, 61–68, 106
   as goal of local church, 41–42
   Corinthian church's failing, 40–41
   deeper dimension of love, 75–76

—M—

Martha, 78
Martin, Glenn, 101
Mary, 7
McGavran, Donald, 95
McIntosh, Gary, 101
Meeting place, 127–28. *See also* Church
   buildings; Finances
Megachurch movement, 24
Members, 57–60
   as members of one another, 60–61
   behavior towards each other, 61–68
   core membership in new church, 129
   fruit of the Spirit, 58–60
   in New Testament, 148–49
   wronging each other, 58.
   See also Local church
Meyers, Marilyn, vii
Millennium, 8
Ministries, 115
Miracles
   in churches, 54
   miracles of Christ, 79
Missionaries, in first century, 15
Missionary church planting, 136–40
Missions, 136–40. *See also* Church
   planting

Additional books from the Swindoll Leadership Library

ANGELS, SATAN, AND DEMONS
Dr. Robert Lightner

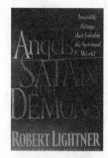

The supernatural world is getting a lot of attention these days in books, movies, and television series. But what does the Bible say about these other-worldly beings? Dr. Robert Lightner answers these questions with an in-depth look at the world of the "invisible" as expressed in Scripture.

THE CHURCH
Dr. Ed Hayes

This important volume explores the labyrinths of the church—delving into her histories, doctrines, rituals, and resources to uncover what it means to be the body of Christ on earth. Both passionate and precise, the essential work offers solid insights on the church's worship, persecution, mission, renewal, and power.

COLOR OUTSIDE THE LINES
Dr. Howard G. Hendricks

All of us yearn to be creative, but few of us feel we truly are. In this fun-to-read, energy-packed volume of the Swindoll Leadership Series, Hendricks proposes a nine-step process for unleashing an exciting spark of creativity and innovation in our lives and ministry. Includes numerous creative approaches to problem solving.

EFFECTIVE CHURCH GROWTH STRATEGIES
Dr. Joseph Wall and Dr. Gene Getz

Effective Church Growth Strategies outlines the biblical foundations necessary for raising healthy churches. Wall and Getz examine the groundwork essential for church growth, qualities of biblically healthy churches, methods for planting a new church, and steps for numerical and spiritual growth. The authors' study of Scripture, history, and culture will spark a new vision for today's church leaders.

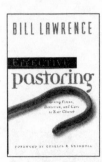

EFFECTIVE PASTORING
Dr. Bill Lawrence

In *Effective Pastoring,* Dr. Bill Lawrence examines what it means to be a pastor in the 21st century. Lawrence discusses often-overlooked issues, writing transparently about the struggles of the pastor, the purpose and practice of servant leadership, and the roles and relationships crucial to pastoring. In doing so, he offers a revealing look beneath the "how to" to the "how to be" for pastors.

EMPOWERED LEADERS
Dr. Hans Finzel

Is leadership really about the rewards, excitement and exhilaration? Or the responsibilities, frustrations and exhausting nights? Dr. Hans Finzel takes readers on a journey into the lives of the Bible's great leaders, unearthing powerful principles for effective leadership in any situation.

END TIMES
Dr. John F. Walvoord

Long regarded as one of the top prophecy experts, Dr. John F. Walvoord now explores world events in light of biblical prophecy. Dealing with every area of biblical prophecy, this is the definitive work on the end times for all church leaders.

THE FORGOTTEN BLESSING
Dr. Henry Holloman

For many Christians, the gift of God's grace is central to their faith. But another gift—sanctification—is often overlooked. *The Forgotten Blessing* clarifies this essential doctrine, showing us what it means to be set apart, and how the process of sanctification can forever change our relationship with God.

GOD
Dr. J. Carl Laney

Who is God? What does He do? How can I know him better? These are questions every Christian asks at some point. J. Carl Laney presents a practical path to life-changing encounters with the goodness, greatness and glory of our Creator.

THE HOLY SPIRIT
Dr. Robert Gromacki

In *The Holy Spirit,* Dr. Robert Gromacki examines the personality, deity, symbols, and gifts of the Holy Spirit, while tracing the ministry of the Spirit throughout the Old Testament, the Gospel Era, the life of Christ, the Book of Acts, and the lives of modern believers.

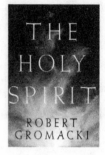

HUMANITY AND SIN
Dr. Robert A. Pyne

Sin may seem like an outdated concept these days, but its consequences remain as destructive as ever. Dr. Robert A. Pyne explores sin's overarching effect on creation and our world today. Learn about the creation of humankind, mankind's sinful nature, and God's plan for the fallen world.

IMMANUEL
Dr. John A. Witmer

Dr. John A. Witmer presents the almighty Son of God as a living, breathing, incarnate man. He shows us a full picture of the Christ in four distinct phases: the Son of God before He became man, the divine suffering man on Earth, the glorified and ascended Christ, and the coming King.

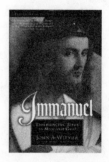

A LIFE OF PRAYER
Dr. Paul Cedar

Dr. Paul Cedar explores prayer through three primary concepts, showing us how to consider, cultivate, and continue a lifestyle of prayer. This volume helps readers recognize the unlimited potential and the awesome purpose of prayer.

MINISTERING TO TODAY'S ADULTS
Dr. Kenn Gangel

After forty years of research and experience, Dr. Kenn Gangel knows what it takes to reach adults for Christ. In an easy-to-understand and apply style, Gangel offers proven systematic strategies for building dynamic adult ministries in the local church.

MORAL DILEMMAS
J. Kerby Anderson

J. Kerby Anderson presents a penetrating volume of solid, practical answers to some of the most perplexing issues facing our society today—issues such as abortion, euthanasia, cloning, capital punishment, genetic engineering, and the environment.

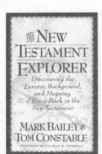

THE NEW TESTAMENT EXPLORER
Dr. Mark Bailey and Dr. Tom Constable

The New Testament Explorer provides a concise, on-target map for traveling through the New Testament. The reader is guided through the New Testament, providing an up-close and to-the-point examination of each paragraph of Scripture and the theological implications of the truths revealed. A great tool for teachers and pastors alike, this book comes equipped with outlines, narrative discussions, and applicable truths for teaching and for living.

SALVATION
Earl D. Radmacher

God's ultimate gift to His children is salvation. In this volume, Earl Radmacher offers an in-depth look at the most fundamental element of the Christian faith. From defining the essentials of salvation to explaining the result of Christ's sacrifice, this book walks readers through the spiritual meaning, motives, application, and eternal result of God's work of salvation in our lives.

SPIRIT-FILLED TEACHING
Dr. Roy B. Zuck

Acclaimed teacher Roy B. Zuck reveals how teachers can tap into the power of divine energy to fulfill their calling and use their gifts at a deeper level. By applying these timeless, spirit-focused principles, teachers will learn how to teach more effectively and inspire students to live out God's word.

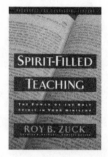

TALE OF THE TARDY OXCART AND 1501 OTHER STORIES
Dr. Charles R. Swindoll

In *The Tale of the Tardy Oxcart*, Charles Swindoll shares from his life-long collection of his and others' personal stories, sermons, and anecdotes. 1501 various illustrations are arranged by subjects alphabetically for quick-and-easy access. A perfect resource for all pastors and speakers.

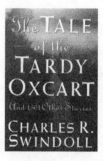

WOMEN AND THE CHURCH
Dr. Lucy Mabery-Foster

Women and the Church provides an overview of the historical, biblical, and cultural perspectives on the unique roles and gifts women bring to the church, while exploring what it takes to minister to women today. Important insight for any leader seeking to understand how to more effectively minister to women and build women's ministries in the local church.